COUNTERING VIOLENCE

Countering Violence

G. N. Devy

Orient BlackSwan

COUNTERING VIOLENCE

ORIENT BLACKSWAN PRIVATE LIMITED

Registered Office
3-6-752 Himayatnagar, Hyderabad 500 029, Telangana, India
e-mail: centraloffice@orientblackswan.com

Other Offices
Bengaluru, Bhopal, Chennai, Guwahati, Hyderabad,
Jaipur, Kolkata, Lucknow, Mumbai,
New Delhi, Noida, Patna, Visakhapatnam

First published by Orient BlackSwan in 2019

029939

ISBN 978-93-5287-660-0

Typeset in
Calisto MT 10/13
by Manmohan Kumar, Delhi

Printed in India at
Glorious Printers, Delhi

Published by
Orient Blackswan Private Limited,
3-6-752 Himayatnagar,
Hyderabad 500 029, Telangana, India
e-mail: info@orientblackswan.com

This work is dedicated to all those thinkers,
from civilisations past and present,
who upheld the principle of non-violence
and gave their all in its defence.

Contents

Introduction ix

1. Countering Violence 1

2. Kikiyario 56
   Adivasi Voice and Violence

3. The Birth of Dakshinayan 89
   Indian Writers in Resistance

Postscript 138

Index 142

Introduction

The centuries during which the world moved towards a pervasive dependence on machine production have arguably also been the centuries that generated a tendency towards violence on a scale unmatched in human history. Mechanised wars, beginning with firearms and moving on to nuclear weapons and chemical arsenal, form but a small portion of the violence generated during these centuries. There was also colonisation, which led to the deportation, displacement, and genocide of the indigenous; an excessive dependence on Reason, wiping out space for Imagination; recourse to writing and printing, negating all that was sacred and authentic in oral traditions; 'development', which acquired the form of majoritarian projects, annihilating minorities; and globalisation, which made the State incapable of compassion for the deprived communities. These centuries have unfolded a theatre of worrisome decline, or even the demise, of irrationality, faith, voice, language, difference, and diversity. In the wake of this multiple assault on human communities, thought, culture, and the symbiotic connect with nature, the very 'nature' of humans appears to have undergone a fundamental transformation, giving violence and what Gandhi would have termed its synonym, greed, a primacy in the ecology of thought.

The transformation appears to have been so fundamental that what was considered ghastly violent action or thought just a few decades ago has now been normalised, and reappears in every decade. Thus, the unimaginable horror invoked by the very idea of a nuclear conflict made traditional wars look like manageable episodes of arms-clash, the subject of a half-semester case study project at a business school; and the rise of non-State party terrorism made the Cold War seem like mere propaganda, part of a semester course at a media school. State surveillance of their own citizens, with the help of artificial intelligence and the associated power of intimidation that these mindless-yet-thinking machines possess, often make the victim societies look back at history with longing and nostalgia, even for the medieval feudal anarchy. In short, the ever-increasing violence has been the backbone of human history over the past half-a-millennium. It is difficult to decide if this has been the case forever in known history; indeed, if being human has perhaps also meant internalising this ever-growing scale of violence. Yet, it cannot be denied that the tendency towards violence has increased enormously through the eras in which rationality, knowledge, capital, and machine, together—and contrary to the rhetoric justifying their emergence—have gained a stranglehold over human society.

Predictably, just as industrial capitalism produced its critique in Karl Marx's utopian ideas, violence aggravated by modernity found its critique in Gandhi's utopian idealism. Not surprisingly, therefore, non-violence became for Gandhi a non-negotiable element of his idea of freedom. Just as various shades of Marxism can be detected in every struggle for equality in modern times—and how seamlessly they can be applied to such struggles before Marx as well—it is also possible to attribute Gandhi's notion of non-violence to all struggles for freedom, including those that preceded him. The logical fallacy and anachronism involved in such attempts notwithstanding, it must be admitted that Gandhi, like Marx, was pointing to something truly fundamental about what has been happening to humans over the past half-a-millennium. Curiously enough, both Marx and Gandhi held the rather simplistic belief that human greed can be contained, if not eliminated altogether, by bringing in, at least as an interim measure, the agency of the State (for Marx) and the conscience or the inner voice (for Gandhi). Both argued against the arrogance of the State, hubris, and left it to individuals to strengthen society through action. It is not my intention to argue that the two were alike in their thought—they certainly were not. I invoke them here to point out that the moral and political responsibility that they place upon individuals is the take-off point for this book.

Countering Violence was not designed from its very beginning as a book. It evolved alongside my personal evolution as a social being over the past five decades. Born in the years immediately following the Partition of India and the assassination of Mahatma Gandhi, I grew up on a liberal diet of contemporary folklore replete with heart-wrenching stories of displaced individuals and charred homes. But I must confess that at that stage, I had not fully grasped their full implications and meaning. My response was compassionate, but perhaps abstract. During the 1960s, India faced two military actions, one on the northern front and the other on its western front. For the new nation, given its inadequate military preparedness, these armed conflicts were a great economic challenge, as much as they were an ideological challenge. Yet, the experience of these wars was significantly different for states in the south and the east than it was for the Himalayan states, and those in the west such as Rajasthan and Punjab. For the other states, the wars meant daily news of attack or retreat, short supplies of food, and an occasional blackout in some cities like Bombay and Poona. From my location in Maharashtra, the violence that one 'experienced' came filtered through reports and the dead bodies of casualties delivered to remote villages in military vans. It was during the Emergency of India (June 1975–March 1977) that I first started becoming aware that the State can be explicitly violent towards citizens. Until then, I had only read about the great violence of the past in the epics, or about distant nations such as Germany, France, Egypt, and Russia. One had also read about the purges in Stalin's Russia and the whimsical tyranny of dictators in some African countries (for example, Gaafar Nimeiry of Sudan and Idi Amin of Uganda). Yet, as sentences printed on paper, these all seemed remote, rather than immediate or shocking.

For many of my generation, the Emergency lent a material body to the idea of fear generated by a structured violence. As one became sensitive to such manifestations of violence, the occasional communal riots, the harassment forced upon cities by various localised political outfits, the presence of *sena*s, and the increasing nexus between crime and politics started making greater sense as part of the pervasive violence at the heart of the caste–class-ridden society. Throughout the 1970s and 1980s, the theme of violence came to occupy imaginative transactions in India. At their best, cinema, theatre, and fiction produced scathing analyses of the causes of violence, seen, for instance, in the works of M. Sathyu (*Garam Hawa*), Shyam Benegal (*Nishant*), Vijay Tendulkar (*Gidhade*), and Mahasweta Devi (*Hajar Churashir Ma*). Yet, in most popular films and fiction, disturbingly violent scenes became a part of the setting—for instance, in the hugely successful film, *Sholay*. Possibly, deep within the minds of the consumers of such works, violence was becoming a seductive merchandise, to be bought and consumed in order to keep their own sense of well-being intact, a kind of modern *catharsis*.

The genocidal attacks on Sikhs in 1984, the demolition of the Babari Masjid in Ayodhya in Uttar Pradesh in December 1992, and subsequent communal violence in numerous towns in 1993 brought the experience of visible violence to the doorsteps of urban Indians. Ethnic and caste identity politics spewing hatred, the spread of Naxalism and communal tensions, and an already failing 'green' revolution brought this violence to the farms and rural hinterlands. This was when the Indian economy was liberalised, initially leading to euphoria, but then slowly cutting into its cultural fabric marked by diversity and the social fabric characterised by tolerance. The 1990s turned India into a perfect site for various manifestations of violence—ecological, economic, social, cultural, ethnic, and communal. Having, by then, published a couple of books, I decided to make a modest attempt to make sense of the violence surrounding me and proposed a study of violence as my chosen theme when a Jawaharlal Nehru Fellowship was awarded to me in 1994.

My initial design for the Fellowship was a typically academic drawing board exercise. It had a schedule of interviews with prisoners charged with homicide or convicted of murders, an elaborate questionnaire, and a fairly long bibliography of articles and books that I had to read in order to understand what other scholars had proposed earlier. I kept to the design quite rigorously for a year and a half. But by 1995, I had started gravitating towards a study of oral traditions and adivasi communities. These topics required my visiting adivasi villages in Gujarat and Maharashtra. Those visits, my conversations with adivasis, and my growing unease with formal education, more specifically the pretentious production of knowledge, brought me to the decision of moving out of formal academics altogether. As my interactions with the adivasis increased, I realised how utterly necessary it was for me to free myself from the idea of 'knowledge as written'. Given the increasing intensity of that thought, I decided to stop reading books—not a sensible decision, but one I found necessary to make at that stage in my work.

This decision entailed an immediate consequence for my project on violence. My daily engagement with adivasis, villages, and the vast machinery of exploitation and deprivation set all around them made me look at violence as a lived experience, rather than as narratives emerging through testimony and anecdotes. It was so much a part of the backdrop throughout my work with adivasis that I no longer found it necessary to consciously 'study' it. Although the notes I had made from all of the books piled on my desk back in Baroda were intact, I started depending more on reflection than on verified logical links gleaned from textual sources. All of this, the reflections and the stock of notes, came in handy when, at the turn of the century, the National Institute of Design, Ahmedabad, asked me to deliver a series of lectures in 1998. These lectures were purely oral and not based on written texts. A few among the audience made copious notes, and Rohini Mokashi-Punekar, who used to teach English at the National Institute of Design at that time and was present for the lectures, compiled the notes. I went through them and rearranged a lot of the material. Since I had started writing in Marathi, I produced an independent draft in Marathi, too. The Marathi text was published in my book *Vanaprastha* (2007), under the title 'Hinse-chi Swapna-srishti' ('The dream world of violence'). The English text—not an exact translation of the Marathi—was published in *The G. N. Devy Reader* (2009), under the title 'Countering Violence'.

I have chosen to place that text in this book as the opening chapter. It explains what 'violence' is by revisiting several prominent theoretical views, spread over disciplines as diverse as psychology, philosophy, the sociology of deviant behaviour, criminology, theology, and history. At the time I wrote it, I had thought that it would be useful for students and scholars interested in understanding violence. As I read it now, I realise that I probably wrote it to enhance my own understanding of the phenomenon. The sequence of arguments and the logic I have employed in developing my thesis are along the lines of some of the ancient Indian theses, which fully develop a certain strand of thought only to show its inadequacy, moving on to another, and yet another. My thesis in the chapter does not seek to uphold any particular analysis or theory of violence. Rather, it states that no understanding helps unless it generates action towards containing violence. The chapter is based on the idea that constructive action is superior to any conceptual formulation of non-violence. On reading it again from a time distance of nearly two decades, I realise that my discussion of violence is devoted to making the world less violent; it is an attempt to escape abstraction and an invitation to action towards containing violence. Hence the title, 'Countering Violence'.

Chapter 2 is reproduced from a book of reflective essays that I published under the title *A Nomad Called Thief* (2011). Before I comment on its contents, let me say that I have not visited Auschwitz. I had read about it, and based my impressions on what I could imagine with the help of reports, history books, and narratives. In 1992, when I was at Yale University on a Fellowship, Professor Geoffrey Hartman asked me to attend a conference he had organised on the 'Future of Memory'. It was devoted to discussing the vast corpus of testimonies of victims of the Holocaust. As I listened to speaker after speaker recalling the horrors of fascism and the concentration camps, I realised that the memory of the traumatised victims and witnesses of violence calls for a completely different understanding from what psychology as a curative practice can offer. It requires not merely a cure and a restoration of the devastated past, but an assurance that the future can be safeguarded. This somewhat vague formulation of mine was further strengthened when, later, I visited the concentration camp site preserved as a museum of public conscience at Sachenhausen. The technical perfection of the horror camp also brought home to me the utter separation of ethics and knowledge in our technology-dominated world. These thoughts resurfaced in my mind as I witnessed the ghastly communal riots of 2002 in Gujarat.

I did not go to Gujarat in 2002 to study the riots or report on them. I just happened to be there, having chosen Gujarat for my domicile since 1980. I could not have escaped being a witness to the rage and the wretchedness of the perpetrators. As the unending violence continued to shake Gujarat and the very foundations of the idea of the state as the guardian of citizen rights, life, and property, I was, like millions of others in Gujarat, able to see the poison of communal hatred, insidiously sown over several decades, erupting into violence of an unusual order. It did not spare even the districts in the east where adivasi communities had been living, until then in isolation. '*Kikiyari*', which in the local speech means a wild-cry, is used by the adivasis in exceptional circumstances. The violent riots of 2002 were no doubt an exceptional situation for them. The plural of the word, '*kikiyario*', is the title of Chapter 2. It chronicles about three weeks of the riots. The chapter describes the circumstances that compelled me to chronicle the events. I had prepared a far more elaborate report; however, only a part of it survived, while the rest could not be traced due to a mix-up with my papers. It was published in *Seminar* in May 2002. Subsequently, I decided to include it in *A Nomad Called Thief*. Following the theoretical Chapter 1, such a chronicle of violence should offer a greater credence to my call for constructive action to counter violence.

The 2002 riots did not leave only Gujarat changed; they also altered the political dynamics in the rest of the country, culminating in a complete control of power by the right-wing government in the Gujarat Assembly elections held in November 2002, and later, in the 2014 elections to the Parliament. The atmosphere generated during this shift led to unchecked attempts at intimidation and the forced suppression of ideas and thoughts defending rationality, scientific temper, tolerance, and a diversity of opinion. This new form of violence manifested itself in the killings of several thinkers, journalists, and persons with dissenting views or ways of life. Based on my understanding of violence, I found it necessary to think of peaceful ways of countering it. The Dakshinayan movement of writers, artists, filmmakers, and thinkers that sprung up as a result is the subject of Chapter 3. The chapter offers a factual account of the genesis of the movement. It also describes the nature of the action possible in times of hubris, hegemony, and a widespread tendency towards violence in word and work. The chapter is a first-person account of the movement from its inception, to the point when it received massive support from the international community of writers, when PEN International asked me to convene the PEN Congress in India. The PEN Congress was held to coincide with the 150th birth anniversary of Mahatma Gandhi (2018–19). It was inaugurated at the memorial of Kasturba Gandhi at Aga Khan Palace, the prison house where she died. My report on Dakshinayan was published in Pune for limited circulation as a booklet. I have used it here.

I have added a brief postscript to the three chapters placed together in this book. It was a piece occasioned by my visit to a public arts installation at the Michigan University campus in Ann Arbor. The installation, on a street either ironically or as a strange coincidence called 'Liberty Street', had thousands of books spread out, with a rather casually placed sign inviting people to trample upon them. Some distance from this site is the magnificent building of Michigan University's main library. The installation was a stark reminder of the 'burning of books' by Hitler's thought police outside Berlin University in 1932. The text offered here as a postscript is built upon an article I contributed to *The Telegraph* in November 2018.

My description of the genesis of each chapter should make it clear that this book was not designed as a single scholarly text. It contains texts that resulted out of my deep engagement with thought and action related to the question of violence over the past several decades. Their unity lies in the unbroken link between my thoughts and action, thoughts about unravelling the human recourse to violence and action to counter violence where I saw it and where I could act. I have brought these essays and texts together in the hope that reading them may strengthen the reader's resolve to make this world less violent. I believe that we can if we learn to value fearlessness and to contain greed. As Gandhi famously said, the self is where a beginning has to be made if we want to see any change.

Countering Violence

Violence

The concepts of race, region, language, and religion are the foremost factors behind the conflicts and massacres in the history of humankind. The pages of history have, time after time, been coloured by the destruction of other communities in the effort to retain the continuity and purity of a race. Numerous examples in history show that individuals who make tremendous sacrifices for the sake of their people are also able, without qualms, to strangulate and make extinct entire communities belonging to other races. Many tricks and ploys are necessary to acquire land, either a tiny piece or a large area. One such trick is to produce weapons, initially to kill other species of animals, and then develop sophisticated weapons in order to destroy other weapon-bearing communities of people. A second is to enforce such rules and laws that restrict the freedom of individuals. An extreme variation of such rules is the construction of systems, especially the political system, which, century by century, tightens the noose around individual cultural independence. The main factor behind violence is the inversely proportional ratio of limited land resource against the multiplying human populations.

Although languages have come into being as a means to conduct our affairs and communicate feelings, and while it is possible to express not only physical sensation but also mental processes beyond these, it is language that sometimes severs communication. As geographical conditions change and mutate, the fertility of the soil dips or increases, and hills, rivers, and forests define the distribution of land, language too changes its nuances and shades of meaning, and from one language emerge several secondary (ancillary) languages and dialects. Economic, political, and cultural factors lead to so many upheavals and changes between one language and another, that it becomes impossible to have only one language in the world. Human communities speaking numerous variations of thousands of languages weld completely the language they speak to the identity of their community. Inevitably, the struggle for their identity gives rise to linguistic misunderstandings.

However, over and above the three factors of race, land, and language, it is religion that contributes the highest proportion of conflict and war. Communities that keep alive conceptions of gods and the modes of their worship do not hesitate to massacre other traditions, destroy their places of worship, and uproot all other conceptions of the divine that seem to challenge their own concept of God. Such acts have been performed with great regularity and dedication throughout human history.

It is not very difficult to discern that these causes of violence—nation, religion, language, and race—also give rise to the most generous and noble sentiments. Men and women who love their country and religion, take pride in their language, and are intimately connected with their race become, in every culture and society, the object of praise and appreciation of their fellow men and women. In short, the inspiration to love and sacrifice, and all emotions noble and ideal, and, as opposed to these, the impulse towards anger, hatred, prejudice, and a desire to smash and break, emotions producing violence, both spring forth from a common source.

The twentieth century will go down as the most violent in the history of mankind. The invention of destructive arms and weapons, their actual use in human destruction, the production of chemicals aimed at the annihilation of entire races, the use of medical means to kill countless people in concentration camps, the engineering of world wars, the kindling and inciting of battles, the banishing of communities to foreign lands and their massacre, schemes that lead to murder and mayhem within a country, the inciting of riots, political assassinations, plunder, and arson—the narrative of violence is filled to an unprecedented degree with the paradoxes of individual criminal tendencies, murder, suicide, and continual imbalances in peace of mind.

Why is it that so much violence has sprung up in the twentieth century? The same century has seen unsurpassed attempts to make human life happier, easier. Cures for many diseases, the invention of amazingly varied means of transportation, freedom from much manual labour, the spread of education and the broadening of knowledge, the end of dictatorial regimes in many nations and the establishment of democracies therein, the ousting of monarchies, wonderful inventions in agriculture, the setting up of factories capable of enormous production, the creation of innumerable devices of entertainment; such admirable and historically incomparable milestones, too, have been achieved in infinitely greater proportions in the twentieth century than in any other.

How can these almost miraculous accomplishments and the unbearable pain brought about by violence be linked? Between these two scripts of happiness and suffering, which is the more authentic script in which the history of the twentieth century can be written? Several books of translation have the convention of publishing poems in the original language on the verso page, with the translated version on the recto page. If the history of the twentieth century—in fact, the history of all centuries—is structured in this composite narrative of construction and destruction, then the transition from the constructive to the destructive becomes impossible to understand. It becomes necessary, therefore, to examine the chemistry of violence. It is essential to impartially observe the mutual relationship between the two worlds of violence: the world of reality and the world of fantasy.

Moral philosophy and ethics regard brutality as an innate tendency constituting a permanent threat to the balance of the mind. Jurisprudence, basing itself on ethics, considers violent deeds abhorrent and institutes State punishment as a deterrent. Medical science believes that the propensity for violent acts is a result of a genetic disorder. Violence is considered a perverse tendency in sociology and is examined independently by criminology, a related field of study. Criminology, besides studying the forms of crimes and their sources, also explores the possible solutions to lessening crime in society. Scholars believe, 'The scholarly objective of criminology is the development of a body of knowledge regarding this process of law, crime and reaction to crime .... The practical objective of criminology, supplementing the scientific or theoretical objective, is to reduce the amount of pain and suffering in the world.'[1]

Since the prime purpose of criminology is to root out pain and suffering in human society, it considers criminal tendencies anti-social. It also lays down certain principles proposing that the structure of the body, the jaw, the shape of the lips, and the colour of the eyes of such anti-social individuals differ from those of other individuals. If the sociologist Eysenck[2] formulated the theory that individuals with criminal tendencies are either extremely gregarious or extremely whimsical and inhibited, Karl A. Menninger believed that criminals are psychotic patients with psychological disorders.[3]

The study of criminal tendencies from the perspective of the shape and proportions of the brain, parts of which may show unexpected growth, as well as of the genetic history of individuals, has been progressing in crime-riddled USA. Some of the conclusions reached by these studies are that the eruption of violent tendencies is dependent on secretions in the brain and their chemical action and reaction. In the February 1994 issue of *New Scientist*, the following comment was made on 'Positive Aggression':

> Except for a few extreme cases nobody has yet proved that damage to a specific part of the brain can be linked to a violent personality. But there is plenty of other evidence linking violence to changes within the brain. Levels of serotonin appear to be lower in the brains of people with violent histories, just as they are in overly pugnacious animals .... Serotonin, the theory goes, might act to suppress impulsive behaviour, and those with less of it in key parts of their brains might be more aggressive as a result.[4]

Neurology notes some instances of aggression of violent emotions due to an unusual fluctuation in substances such as dopamine and serotonin. Although it is possible to come to some general conclusions from these sciences about the individual propensity to violence, to assume that the overflow of certain chemicals produces violence, or that those persons with large heads, eyes or lips, or those who are talkative, all perform violent deeds are conclusions that cannot be held.

It is true that violence is socially destructive, and that violence and crime have to be curbed, but it is equally true that it is still not possible even to diagnose, however superficially, the condition of the mind in which the roots of violence have deeply entrenched themselves.

In World War II, the Nazi government of Germany reduced the Jews to unimaginably dire conditions. The attempt was to stamp them out by terrible, brutal means. Many historians and thinkers have since written and debated copiously about the violence during this war, Hannah Arendt being one of the foremost amongst them.[5] According to her, the Jews had been ill-treated in Europe even before World War II. In the nineteenth century, an ideal example of this would be the Dreyfus case. Although in fact innocent, Dreyfus, a Jewish army official, was accused of spying against France and sentenced to death by hanging. French novelist and journalist Emile Zola ran a protest campaign against this for years on end and forced the government to annul the sentence; however, French citizens continued to look upon Jews as murderers and traitors. In Russia, too, the campaign to annihilate Jews had been in practice from earlier times, and gained greater strength during the communist political regime of Stalin.

It is against this background that Hitler achieved political power with his anti-Jewish propaganda. Putting the propaganda into practice, he mercilessly murdered millions of Jews. According to Hannah Arendt, the Jews in Europe had prosperity but no political power, and when, in any society, there is a wide disparity among a section between its economic power and political power, there are bound to be violent attacks on that group. There can be an opposite theory for India: here, there are continuous violent attacks on a section of society that has a share in political power, but absolutely no place in economic power. Although both theories seem apparently convincing, they cannot hold true for all societies and all epochs in history. During the French Revolution, even when both economic prosperity and political power were combined in the hands of one class of society, that class had to confront tremendous social aggression. As opposed to this, in medieval India the untouchable caste, which had no political power and no economic prosperity, was the victim of a terrible violent oppression. From the above, it can be said that while Hannah Arendt's conclusions are true for a particular period in the history of Germany, they cannot be accepted as universally true for all violent transactions.

Sociology generally uses economic reasons to explain individual instances of violence and criminal tendencies. In a very important volume, *Deviant Behaviour,* Robert Merton traces the two-way process behind anti-social deeds—poverty and the stifling of opportunities in individual economic development:

> Poverty is not an isolated variable. It is one in a complex of interdependent social and cultural variables ... only insofar as poverty and associated disadvantages in competition for the cultural values approved for all members of the society are linked with the assimilation of cultural emphasis on monetary accumulation as a symbol of success is antisocial conduct a 'normal' outcome .... It is only when the full configuration is considered, poverty, limited opportunity and a commonly shared system of success symbols that we can explain the higher association between poverty and crime in our country.[6]

In Merton's view, it is not poverty alone that is the reason for crime; when economic prosperity and social success are linked together, it is at that point that crime takes birth in poverty. That is, Merton has an economic perspective in his analysis of criminal violence. However, it is quite clear that while the economic angle cannot be kept away from an analysis of violence, the predisposition to kick out at cats and dogs when simply walking past, to crush insects underfoot, to pluck at branches and leaves without any reason—such violence upon natural flora and fauna, innocent of any economic interest, does not figure in Merton's theories. Although, when two countries are at war with each other, the cause behind the colossal destructive activity may be economic, it is hardly likely that the feelings of violence in the minds of the soldiers engaged in warfare arises from an ongoing examination of the economic condition of their respective countries.

Emile Durkheim argued that in every period and every form of economic and historical system, violence and crime have appeared continuously:

> Crime is present not only in the majority of societies of one particular species but also in all societies of all type. There is no society that is not confronted with the problem of criminality. Its form changes; the

> acts thus characterized are not the same everywhere; but everywhere and always, there have been men who have behaved in such a way as to draw upon themselves penal repression.[7]

As a particular society achieves economic development, violent aggressions increase in that society. According to Durkheim, crime had increased by 300 per cent in nineteenth-century France. As such, instead of understanding criminality as a social perversity, it may be better to consider it an indivisible part of social living. It is perhaps the inevitable result of the innate cunning in the human species. Yet, deciding what crimes should be deemed punishable changes in every age in a society. A deed sentenced with retribution in a particular age may be considered innocent in a succeeding age; or, conversely, acts considered blameless in one age can be declared criminal in another. Obviously, the scales evaluating crime and violence change continually. From the perspective of the time-bound nature of criminal law and punitive measures, it may be observed that it is impossible to define violence or crime in the absence of a time framework. Human sacrifices made for the appeasement of some gods in a specific period are understood to be the handiwork of Satan in another epoch. It cannot, therefore, be concluded that human sacrifice has been universally condemned. Furthermore, it is possible that there exist different rules for punishment in different societies in the same time period. A given society may unanimously agree upon the severing of limbs as punishment for crime; however, another society of the same time may consider this inhuman. It can be said, therefore, that although punishing criminal acts is a universal custom, a universal matrix for crime and punishment is not available, nor is it easy to understand what crime and punishment really are. In Durkheim's opinion, even if, at some point in time, should there be a society of exemplary individuals, perhaps the most trivial of mistakes would shock such a society, and thus even nominal faults would be punished:

> Imagine a society of saints, a perfect cloister of exemplary individuals. Crimes, properly so-called, will there be unknown; but faults, which appear venial to the layman, will create there the same scandal that the ordinary offence does in ordinary consciousness. If, then, this society has the power to judge and punish, it will define these acts as criminal and will treat them as such.[8]

One can only conclude from the above that notions of crime and violence exist in every society; however, the interpretation and definition of these notions are embedded within the framework of culture and time. It is not possible for every individual within a society to don all the identical expressions and gestures of the common collective mask of that society. There will be at least a few individuals who see differently, and who hold opinions different from the apparently common mask that a social structure engenders. As a result, such individuals are perceived as anti-social or perverse by that society. This implies that in the indistinguishable relationship between individual and society, the dark animal instinct for violence is a permanent bylane which every society forever tries, from within itself, to block and stifle.

But any society, in the interest of progress, is always unquestioningly in need of anti-social persons who forge ever-new bylanes in this relation between the individual and society. Every social reformer opposes established social norms and brings forward new thoughts and new ways of conducting life. The scientist Galileo or the saint Tukaram were treated almost as criminals by their contemporaries. Human societies seem to progress on the principle embodied in the words of Durkheim, 'Nothing is good indefinitely and to an unlimited extent'. Socrates was declared a criminal by the laws of Athens. Jesus Christ was crucified for his 'criminality' and beside him, nailed to a second cross, was a thief, one whom we would still consider a criminal. Every individual who has been declared a criminal by her/his society has attempted to transgress established rules of conduct and, to that extent, is an original thinker. Obviously, radical thinkers and social reformers on the one hand and criminals and persons of violent tendencies on the other cannot both be measured on the same scale. Even so, in order to produce thoughts that modify and change the shape and contour of society, it is necessary to have an unlimited harvest of what might, at any given moment, be considered anti-social acts. According to the theories of Durkheim, in the lush undergrowth of anti-social ideas and deeds, somewhere the huge trees of visionaries take root and vigour:

> To make progress, individual originality must be able to express itself. In order that the originality of the idealist whose dreams transcend his century may find expression, it is necessary that the originality of the criminal, who is below the level of his time, shall also be possible. One does not occur without the other.[9]

Visionaries such as Socrates, Christ, Galileo, and Tukaram take shape from a shadowy world of ideas and dreams outside the accepted parameters of society. According to Durkheim, it is this very space that also spawns the criminal. It may be necessary therefore to portray this outer region to understand violence.

The dream world of violence is netted by the crisscrossing strands of latent temptations and terror: there is the wordless possibility of the fulfillment of lust and the temptation of boundless enjoyment of power and economic gain, and the haunting terrors of impotence and of death. Rape, the exploitation of women, and the sexual abuse of minors can be listed under the category of sexual violence. Along with these may be counted the spurts of ordinary anger that lead to barbarism, and abusive language that describes either the desire for physical violence, or sexual violence against the mother/sister of the object of one's anger. If theft, dacoity, murder, arson, and plunders fulfil the lust for money, then the violence that destroys particular sections of society constitutes the lust for power. But the begetters and supporters of such violence are constantly devoured by a fear of their own impotence. A bully or *dada* is, from a psychological perspective, a person living in constant dread of losing his own manhood. This instinctual apprehension of impotence troubles not only individuals, but also suppressed cultures and societies. Beset by this anxiety, they take to extreme violence. The man who kills his wife without any strong economic motive is, in all likelihood, obsessed with the fear of impotence. Similarly, leaders who push a society towards unnecessary violence can also be seen to be deeply troubled by the same fear. Common bullies who set up non-government 'armies' and threaten innocent citizens into advancing protection money live in extreme fear of individual debilitation. There is considerable disparity between the fear of impotence and actual sexual incapacity. This state of mind has no basis in actual physical defect, but is the result of a mental makeup, as 'the impotence is clearly psychological when the anamnesis reveals its selective occurrence'.[10]

Individuals afflicted by this violence generating anxiety, initially start using extremely powerful verbal feats in order to influence their audience. Quite a few among these develop into forceful influential orators and create an oratory that invades, seizes, and hypnotises the listening community. In their field of consciousness, the dividing line between reality and fantasy becomes more and more hazy, and the self-created, novel, dream-like reality is the one they begin to live in. Consequently, their sympathy for the suffering of others diminishes. The road to mass slaughter, and the torture of millions without scruple or qualm is now clear: Adolf Hitler was one such leader.

Hitler spent his childhood in wretched conditions. In his youth, he joined the German army and during World War I, fought on the front. When Germany lost the war and the young boys of the army were let loose without employment or wherewithal, Hitler began to live as a menial in Vienna. He actually wished to be a painter, but circumstances forced him onto a different path. In despair, Hitler began to identify himself with the defeat of Germany. From this identification was born Hitler, the political aspirant. He began to turn the focus of the anger and hatred that he felt for his own life towards the communists and the Jews. This was also the source of his singular oratorical skills. The unprecedented philosophy of violence that he developed emerged from these factors. His hatred for the human species can be seen in his own words:

> Like a woman ... who would rather bow to the strong man than dominate the weakling ... the masses of the people prefer the ruler to the suppliant and are filled with a stronger sense of mental security by a teaching that brooks no rival than by a teaching which offers them a liberal choice .... They feel very little shame at being terrorized intellectually and they are scarcely conscious of the fact that their freedom as human beings is impudently absurd .... They see only the ruthless force and brutality of its determined utterances, to which they always submit.[11]

These conclusions that compare the people with a woman, projecting the image of woman as weak and powerless, and that see a woman as enjoying brutal terrorisation, are an example of the philosophy that reflects Hitler's perverse sexual imagination. This is Hitler at the beginning of his political career. After he had accepted the leadership of his newly formed National Socialist (Nazi) party, there began clashes between the 'non-government' army that he had established and the police troops of the contemporary weak government. In 1923, he was imprisoned in the Landresburg prison for his role in the well-known Munich Beer Hall revolt. During the year of his imprisonment, the young Hitler wrote *Mein Kampf* which is, in effect, a treatise of his political philosophy. In this book is clearly perceived the maturing of his violent scheme of thought. The readers of those times in Germany understood Hitler's ideas to be only political propaganda. No one believed that he himself considered these ideas with any seriousness, or that he would really implement them once he had secured power. Had that happened, perhaps the entire history of the twentieth century would be different. But as *Mein Kampf* shows, Hitler himself felt that the destructive dream world of his thoughts was real; and he also believed implicitly that this fantasy was the new spiritual guiding force of life. The convergence of faith and violence is seen to constantly generate upheavals in history.

> When sheer force is used to combat the spread of a doctrine, then that force must be employed systematically and persistently. This means that the chances of success in the suppression of a doctrine lie only in the persistent and uniform application of the method chosen. The moment hesitation is shown and periods of tolerance alternate with the application of force, the doctrine against which these measures are directed will not only recover strength but every successive persecution will bring to its support new adherents who have been shocked by the oppressive methods employed.[12]

The basic principle underlying Hitler's politics was violence and his image of society was feminine. That the masses in any country are feminine in character and that they are attracted by a show of violent strength were the most important principles in his discourse. Thus, violence became the crucial means of getting and keeping power. No one who was not ready to inflict violence had the right to come to power. Moreover, Hitler's assumption was that he who wished to live must fight: 'He who would live must fight. He who does not wish to fight in this world … has not the right to exist.'[13]

The youth of the vanquished Germany were attracted by Hitler's philosophy of violence. Germany between the two world wars is an excellent example of how an entire society, beset by the fear of impotence, becomes brutal. A whole section of despairing youth, smarting under the humiliation following defeat in the war, was lured into believing Hitler's strident propaganda. Increasingly, reality and fantasy mingled insidiously with each other in Hitler's dream world. Towards the end of his hegemony, even when the fall of Germany was certain and the Allies were on the threshold of Berlin, Hitler was still sending written orders to the fragmented divisions of his annihilated army. Another important aspect of his philosophy was the belief in the glory of untruth. His words in the German tongue are '*In der Groesse der Leregeliegt immer ein Faktor des Geglaubt-werdens*', which may be translated as, 'in every big untruth inheres a confidence begetting quality'. The greater the proportion of untruth, the greater is its ability to evoke trust. As the range of the lie expands, so too does the probability of that land of fantasy.

Hitler presumed that the understanding of the common people, especially the minimum common denominator of their collective intelligence, was very low. Such deficient understanding comprehends only the dangerously easy language of violence. The message that he gave to wartime Germany was couched in similar simple words: Do or die. Those who would not surrender to this apostle of violence would have to accept death. In the name of genetic identity, for the sake of retaining the purity of race, Hitler's forcible transgression of civil society, originating from a fear of castration, was the most shameful of all the orgies of violence unleashed in history by a power-hungry leader. Obviously there continue to be, even after Hitler, many such orgies of violence, unknown to history in the small bylanes of every big city.

Fear of Death: East and West

Not all violence stems from the fear of impotence, however; much stronger is the fear of death. When conflicts and differences arise between families or communities, even ordinarily peaceful individuals are likely to turn violent. The main cause of this appears to be the fear of mortality. In the name of self-defence, human beings have kept up with their business of killing other animals. Despite being acquainted with a bookish knowledge of snakes, if a person was to be confronted with a non-venomous reptile, his first, uncontrollable instinct would be to kill it. Such instances of the fear of death may be observed in violent behaviour.

While critically evaluating tragedy, the most dominant form of literature in ancient Greece, Aristotle came upon the understanding that the watching spectators keenly felt two predominant emotions: fear and pity. When spectators see even the powerful and the mighty, such as a God or a king, fall in the end to death, they become deeply uneasy at the realisation that there can be no escape from death for anyone. At the same time, however, they also feel a sense of relief in the fact that the loss suffered by the hero is not their own.

As capitalism developed, Western society increasingly privileged the youth. Youth became important because it is, in all senses, productive. Correspondingly, old age and death held more dread. Earlier, in medieval Europe, Hercules, Atlas, King Lear, and such characters of advanced age used to appear as heroes in literature and mythology. But since the utmost value was now placed on youth, a new literary custom evolved—projecting the hero as youthful. The hero of Oscar Wilde's *The Picture of Dorian Gray*, who hankers after perennial youth, is but a representative of capitalist society's dread of old age and death.

The reverberations of the increasing fear of death were felt in Western medical science too. The central preoccupation of Western medicine since the end of the last century has been the attempt to defeat death. Surgical operations—a medical treatment that involves making violent, if curative, incisions on the body, gained both acceptance and impetus. This violence on the human body in Western surgery, together with the violent use of nature in Western technology, are clearly projections of the deeply embedded fear of death.

In Western theology, particularly in Christianity, it is believed that humankind, tainted with original sin, is born with the seed of mortality. Western systems of knowledge founded on such a theology have developed on the most strenuous attempts to obtain victory over death, and as such, violence is woven into the very fabric of these systems. If the physical sciences were ceaselessly utilised to take possession of as much land as possible, to refine arms and weapons, to cross the limits of time and place, seize new regions and societies and castrate them, the main purpose of sociology, economics, and anthropology was to extend the limits of human freedom. In an individualistic society, a system is generated whereby every individual is safe from any kind of division. The word 'individual' in English is, at its root, connected to the indivisible. A capitalist society inevitably depends on all kinds and manner of violence to preserve and keep safe an individual's indivisibility.

Western systems of knowledge, political structure, aesthetics, and psychology have evolved from that basis of Christian theology that focuses on the fear of death and the concept of original sin. All facets of Western life and its intellectual progress are coloured dark by violence. Behind the nineteenth-century colonisation undertaken worldwide by European countries was the support of its philosophy of violence.

As opposed to this, a culture that considers death an ordinary, natural event and whose philosophy establishes the possibility of an afterlife will perhaps lay out a different equation with violence. This different equation may be seen in Indian philosophy in the times of the Mahabharata. Every epic narrates a violent confrontation; but it is difficult to find anywhere in world literature the several different kinds of violence and the profound philosophical thought relating to it that is discussed in the Mahabharata.

The dialogue that the armed and war-weary Arjuna has with Krishna right on the battlefield is embodied in the Bhagawad Gita—a systematic body of all the ideas and notions of violence that have prevailed in Indian culture. In it, and especially in the first two chapters, are discussed several ideas of violence reflected in Western culture and philosophy. Bow and arrow in hand, Arjuna says to Krishna, 'Take me right to the middle of these two seas of army so that I may clearly see all the violent deeds of these warriors' (*Senayor ubhayor madhye sthapayati me Achutd*).[14]

The first two chapters contain repeated references to the endless stretch of columns of soldiers, which ensures that the reader never loses sight of the fact that the entire dialogue of the Gita takes place on the actual battlefield. When Krishna drives Arjuna's chariot to the centre of the two armies, Arjuna's eyes fall on Bhishma, Dronacharya, and the other commanders. He can also see the warriors of the entire Kaurava clan. On seeing all these warriors, his own relatives, kith and kin, Arjuna asks, 'What is the use of killing them? The only thing that will come about is the ruin of this clan.'

Thinking about such a violent end, Arjuna becomes dejected. The thought of this imminent destruction sets his body trembling and he feels that his bow, the Gandiv, would fall from his nerveless fingers. He says to Krishna:

> O Janardan, even if these people, out of greed, do not in the least care that the family will be destroyed, why should we who can think, take part in this massive violence? The loss of family means the loss of family dharma. And I have got ready to commit this enormous sin! The root of this violence lies in the greed for power. I do not wish the power or the violence. It would be better if the sons of Dhritarashtra slay me in an unarmed state: that may be more proper.

Looking at Arjuna in such a condition, Krishna says: 'This despair does not suit you. Shake off this debility.'

Arjuna replies: 'It might be better to beg for my living than kill my guru and gain a kingdom, because if I kill him and win the kingdom, every luxury and joy will be stained with his blood.'

In the entire conversation, the subject of violence is structured in the context of desire, the will to power, impotence, and the fear of death. But violence, as opposed to non-violence, is not the main subject of the Gita. Knowledge—as against ignorance—is the main theme. Standing between the two armies, looking at Arjuna's limp figure, Krishna says,

> Though your words seem to be knowledgeable they are really a product of ignorance. The enlightened one does not fall prey to such shallow sorrows. The truth is that, what is not the truth will not last and that which is eternal will never be destroyed.
>
> No warrior can possibly kill what is eternal. That is why both the one who inflicts hurt and the one who is hurt, are removed from real knowledge. Because that which is without end is neither destructive nor capable of being destroyed.
>
> Hence, O Parth, examine deeply your thoughts on death. Do not fall into a false duel of the killer 'you' and the slain 'they'; though you do not kill them, what is mortal will die. Therefore, without taking credit for any success perform your duty. You cannot

> destroy them by killing only their physical bodies for within them too are the eternal.
>
> On the contrary, if you learn to recognize the eternal truth in all the animal species your sorrow will vanish in a moment. And without crediting success to yourself if you fight and win then happiness will be gained, if you lose you will enter heaven.

It must be noted that in Krishna's advice, there is no glorification of violence. Nor does he tell Arjuna that the body is perishable, and so there is no harm in violence. The gist of his advice is: violence, which is a product of ignorance, is as ignoble as the non-violence that stems from ignorance. Non-violence practised merely out of a fear of destroying the family and violence committed out of a desire to preserve the family are both equally deplorable. Instead, if an individual, through his knowledge of living creatures and the regular functioning of the universe, were to go about his duty in a spirit of detachment, then even necessary violence would be as noble as that necessary non-violence. The important issue is not violence, but consciousness. At this, Arjuna enquires, 'How may a being full of enlightenment be described?'

In the words of Krishna, the one who holds joy and sorrow alike, stays aloof from desire, and can avoid both fear and anger—he is the enlightened one. The one who can separate sense feeling from sense gratification is the conscious one.

Western knowledge, political system, and social structure have grown around the necessity to satisfy the senses. The violence necessary for such satisfaction has been considered acceptable there. In ancient Indian culture, however, the place of knowledge was understood to be higher than that of physical happiness. Western science and technology, attracted by sense gratification, have been seeking, till date, ways of triumphing over death, over nature, and other living creatures. As opposed to this, Indian sciences, philosophy, and technology, without considering death the final experience, without claiming nature as separate from human consciousness or other societies as alien to one's own, and, most importantly, without considering physical gratification to be greater than knowledge, have made their way through the ages. Accordingly, in Western culture, the innate tendency towards violence in the human mind forged an open and external path. Violence, in Indian society, turned inwards, and the coveting of physical joys was suppressed. Therefore, in Indian society, various forms of violence directed towards the self are present at different levels.

At the beginning of the twentieth century, the Gita underwent several new translations, and many new commentaries were made on it. Of these, the two most important are Lokmanya Tilak's *Gita Rahasya* and Aurobindo's *Essays on the Gita.* Tilak believed that the Gita teaches a philosophy of action. Previously, scholars had interpreted the main significance of the Gita as renunciation or knowledge. Although Tilak's commentary made no objection to such an interpretation, he took exception to the view that the Gita focused only on renunciation or that its predominant meaning is knowledge

> I do not say that the Gita has not preached Vedanta or Devotion or the Patanjali Yoga at all. But the combination of these three subjects which has been made by the Gita must be such that thereby Arjuna, who was on the horns of a terrible dilemma of conflicting principles of morality, and who had on that account become so confused about his proper duty as to say: 'Shall I do this, or shall I do that?' could find a sinless path of duty and feel inclined to perform the duties enjoined on him by his status as a warrior. In short, it is perfectly clear that the proper preaching in this place would be of Energism (*pravritti*) and that, as all other things are only supporting Energism, that is, as they are all auxiliary, the purport of the Gita religion must also be to support Energism, that is, to support action.[15]

Tilak based his argument on several fields of scholarship while viewing the Gita as a whole: its location, its principal theme, its effect and its originality, and the theory of existence that could be garnered from it.

Shri Aurobindo attempted to formulate a theory that would enable the human being to find spiritual evolution from the three-streamed unification of the paths of knowledge, renunciation, and action. Arjuna asks Krishna, 'Is the violence committed by me pardonable?' Aurobindo's discussion takes this question into account by addressing two issues. The first is that Arjuna's warfare is in conformity with the dharma of his clan. The second is that Arjun's nature was consistent with his duty. Aurobindo's Krishna answers Arjuna thus,

> This high and great knowledge, this strenuous self-discipline of the mind and soul by which it is to rise beyond the clamour of the emotions and the delusion of the senses to true self-knowledge, may well free us from grief and delusion, it may well cure us of the fear of death and the sorrow for the dead, it may well show us that those whom we speak of as dead are not dead at all nor to be sorrowed for, since they have only gone beyond, it may well teach us to look undisturbed upon the most terrible assaults of life and upon the death of the body as a trifle ....[16]

In order to completely erase Arjuna's dejection, to steady his mind stunned 'by the violence that was taking place before his eyes', Krishna further says,

> If you are not satisfied with your social duty and the virtue of your order, if you think that leads you to sorrow and sin, then I bid you rise to a higher and not sink to a lower ideal. Put away all egoism from you, disregard joy and sorrow, disregard gain and loss and all worldly results; look only at the cause you must serve

and the work that you must achieve by divine command; so thou shalt not incur sin.[17]

Contained in the thought of the Gita is the philosophy of control over the senses. The philosophy of sense gratification, characteristic of Western culture, is diametrically opposed to this. But just as a philosophy of sense gratification gives rise to an illusory, fantasy-ridden world of violence, structured by desire and fear, in like manner, the philosophy of sense control subtly creates another world of violence. In such a world, the realities of life are frozen. The reality of this dream world becomes more important than the empirical reality. As a result, both positive and negative aspects of violence, as well as non-violence come to be negated. This means that in this dream world, the presence or absence of violence makes no difference. Hence, in the actual reality of living, violence gets a free rein. Once this stand is accepted, the moral perspective on killing of the body turns lax.

DEATH BY ORDER

A highly interesting work by historian Upendra Thakur, *The History of Suicide in India*, analyses the typology of suicide in different regions of India and comes to the following conclusions:

> What do these instances point to? Why this colossal indifference towards the most precious thing on earth—life? They clearly show that when there was enough attachment to persons or even to ideas, people ceased to have all interest in life and were prepared to sacrifice it as if it were a trifle.[18]

In the twenty-first century, the number of suicides in India has increased significantly:

> But the staggering figure for suicide in modern India as we know it through daily newspaper and periodicals and other such sources in the absence of any authoritative official statistics collated, collected and compiled for the purpose beat all the previous records hollow.[19] ... But if we take into account all reports on suicides hitherto published in English and other dailies in Indian languages all over the country, the number would be so staggering and horrifying so as to make us shudder.[20]

Like suicide, the looting and killing of people, the burning of young brides, sacrificing human beings in order to propitiate the gods, giving away girl children to temples and later turning them into prostitutes, murdering for trivial enmities, burning the houses of Muslims and Dalits, the blinding of Dalits by responsible government officials, mutilating one's own family members by cutting off an ear or a nose as a 'minor' punishment, self-immolation as protest—examples of such violent deeds abound in India. Just as the fear of death may be the moving force behind violence, so too the understanding that death is not the final and real experience and the less importance to the physical, sensual reality may trigger a different kind of self-absorbed violence. Treason against one's own people, the privileging of the spiritual at the cost of suppressing the sensual, and the continuous caste strife seen in social life are forms of violence in India.

Medical science has attempted to analyse the psychological tendency to inflict violence on the self. Just as violent thoughts increase with the decreased flow of serotonin to the brain, suicidal tendencies, too, gain strength with a limited supply of this chemical. J. John Mann of the Columbia Presbyterian Medical Center propounded this theory after examining several patients.[21] Serotonin keeps the intensity of feelings under check and, as a result, an individual has greater control over his behaviour. As the flow of serotonin inside the brain decreases by 20–25 per cent, an individual starts experiencing either violent or suicidal thoughts. If such individuals are naturally prone to depression, the possibility of suicide is definitely enhanced. Such individuals may also conceal their thoughts from doctors. Dr Mann analysed the psychological states of mind of patients from Finland and England who had attempted to kill themselves, and after verifying that it was a lack of sufficient serotonin that was the chief medical reason for suicide, he put into effect a new method of treatment—PET (Positron Emission Tomography)—in order to lessen the incidence of suicide.

While making use of this treatment, Dr Mann realised that long periods of misery and deprivation in childhood have the effect of reducing the brain's capacity to produce serotonin. Such reduced capacity later becomes a permanent genetic feature of that patient. That is, such unsound states of mind pass from one generation to the next. A whole class of people characterised by a decreased production of serotonin comes into being in a society wracked by poverty, and wretched and deprived childhoods. In addition, suicidal thoughts may become an integral part of common social behaviour. In course of time, such social behaviour and thought find cultural acceptability. In other words, ecological, material, and economic factors contribute in a major way to the emergence of and increase in violence, and also in violence gaining cultural status.

The practice of *sati,* the custom of several widowed women collectively immolating themselves on a common pyre on the death of the king, and giving up on tactical warfare to commit *harakiri* when faced with the certainty of defeat in war came into being as cultural practices and attained spiritual status in Rajasthan, the region that experiences a scarcity of fresh fruit and vegetables. The customs of any society that are given cultural approval initially evolve from the degree of fertility of the soil, the climatic conditions, and the availability of foodgrains. Subsequently, as a result of the cyclical and recurrent nature of history, these customs turn into cultural values, and still later, a philosophy that upholds and nourishes these values gradually forms itself.

At this point, one can shift to another track and examine the discipline of Psychology, which has made numerous attempts to search for the roots of violence in social and economic conditions, in individual mental makeup, in philosophic and spiritual formations, and in the political system of a community. There are thinkers who consider it necessary to examine episodes of violence in order to understand violence, to classify, grade, and arrange them in numerical charts. A specialist in criminal law, Hans Torov, has published a scholarly book titled *Violent Men: An Inquiry into the Psychology of Violence?* (1969), which makes a study along these lines.[22] He lists nine types of violence in this book. Violence arises from the tendencies to subdue by force, the implementation of rule and law, shame and disgrace, self-defence, domination, plunder and robbery, bullying, and the eruption of suppressed feelings. Categories based on such descriptions have their own limitations; they are built on an examination of instances of violence within a particular society, at a particular period of time. In such cataloguing, prisoners locked up in jails, patients with mental health problems in hospitals, and people on the streets of cities are interviewed and questioned by a specific method, after which the information received is classified. Such studies may benefit the police and the judiciary, or those who administer jails or treat the mentally diseased; but beyond this, they are not very useful in understanding the origins and roots of violence.

Psychology examines why certain persons treat their own selves with hostility, inflict torture on themselves, or behave in a diabolical fashion towards others. More particularly, it gauges the mysterious relation between the unconscious and the sense perception. The main premise on which psychology and sociology base themselves is that tendencies towards violence are caused by external circumstances, and these suppressed feelings rise to the surface again due to the force of circumstances. But there is also an opposite analysis of violence that has emerged from the life sciences. This view holds that as the human species evolved gradually from a less intelligent organism, it must have picked up the natural instinct for violence from the less developed species. This involves a sub-principle too: although nature has endowed man with the most powerful weapon of reason, it has given man no sharp nails and teeth, pointed horns, strong tail, heels that enable the owner to run like lightning, the ability to change in a moment the colour of the skin, poisonous fangs, or any other physical means to protect himself. As the human mind developed, violence became the only weapon at its disposal to protect itself. The main argument that can be put forward to support this principle is: very few animals practise killing other members of their own kind; however, in human communities, not only is the killing of other human beings accepted, but it is also considered inevitable, and even honourable. Therefore, it is believed that the human species, which kills its own brethren, is the most brutal and violent of all living creatures in nature.

Although this argument seems reasonable, it is not very difficult to locate its faulty logic. It is true that humans kill each other; but it is also true that human beings run hospitals for others of their kind, find new medicines, shelter the destitute, evolve philosophies to lessen pain and sorrow, create concepts of divinities, and generate religious institutions based on such concepts. One does not see wild animals doing any of these things. But it is also not correct to conclude from the above that the human species is of a more patient nature than other animals. The truth is that the violence in the minds of human beings and in society and the violence in the consciousness of wild animals cannot be measured on the same scale. Because of the gift of language, man is able to speak about his own and other bodies; and as a result, there is a deep chasm between the human point of view of human bodies, and the perspective of developed, but language-less, animals.

Whenever a new word is coined for a thing or an experience in human society, a new distance is created between the object or experience, and the one who experiences it. Until that moment, there were only two entities in nature: the thing itself and the experiences of that thing; but after the inception of the word, there comes into being a triangular relation among the thing, the experiences, and, in the absence of the thing itself, its representative word. Our own names are only words. But with the word, our body (and mind) presents itself before us. That is, a new body/being outside of our body enters our consciousness. As a result, the acute sensitivity to the body gets divided into the actual body and the word-body. There is, therefore, a very profound difference between the violence in human interactions and the violence in the animal world. The process of evolution is not only continuous, but also one of incessant transition. Sometimes these transitions are of such magnitude that the newly created thing may be radically different from its substance prior to the transition. Since language is central to human society, the evolution of violent tendencies in nature need to be understood within this framework of continuity as well as transition.

Two important points arise from the above reflections. First, it is important to be aware that violence appears in different images in every age; second, when violence is set free in the medium of language, violent feelings and deeds, and the means to tolerate violence—aspects involving sense experience—change to a new structure altogether. In short, during the natural evolutionary process, and particularly in the progress of human society, violent emotions and experience emerge out of actual oppression and suffering but progressively transform into commercial products, and a society that is able to create and tolerate violence comes into being. In our time, it is now routine to produce violence in a symbolic form and suppress it in an equally symbolic manner. A political party issues a statement in the newspapers and declares a *bandh*, and the government mans the streets with gun-toting policemen who do not have to fire a single bullet! Such rituals are an indication of the symbolic transaction of the production and management of violence. The killing of a person located thousands of miles away through a mere phone call, and carried out by hired mercenaries, is an indication of the commodification of violence.

DISTANCED VIOLENCE

In very ancient times, violence was an experience of the actual infliction of pain and suffering. Today, it can be bought and sold. Even if it is a reality at the experiential level, its material nature has become more encompassing. The indicators of the sale/bargaining/marketing of violence vary in every society and every epoch. They have their own particular identity. It may also be claimed that as increasingly newer shapes and forms are produced in the text of violence, society too changes into newer forms. From this perspective, it is very difficult to say which comes first: the structure of the society or the rhythm and encasing of violence; because although violence is a constant feature of human civilisation, the type of violence and the society of that time are intricately intertwined. If one were to look at the history of ideas, it may seem as though camps of human society have settled themselves on the banks of violence. From the point of view of law, it seems as though the secret paths of violence have always surprised the world by making sudden social appearances. Physiology and medicine only declare the exact moment when violence was inflicted on the body, while economics and political science reiterate its inevitability. Psychology has made the closest study of violence, yet the general confusion in this discipline about what constitutes a 'normal' state of mind leads to an expected confusion in its understanding of violence. Moreover, it is clear that psychology will be unable to throw much light on the material aspects of violence. Perhaps it may be more appropriate to speak through metaphor and simile, and describe violence in the way the Brahma of Advaita is defined, in terms of *neti neti*, or what it is not.

The French Revolution (1789–99) attempted to overthrow the exploitative rule of the Louis dynasty. Soon after, women, men, and children of this family, as well as the nobles and aristocrats faithful to them, were publicly executed by the guillotine. In a few years, taking advantage of the unstable political situation caused by the Revolution, Napoleon Bonaparte, a young army officer, rose to power and conquered Austria, Prussia, Italy, and other countries. For twenty-five years, between 1791 and 1815, Napoleon's ambitions led to a number of wars being fought in Europe, in which thousands of innocent people lost their lives. During the Revolution and later, while the wars were fought, the French people dreamt of a new world; and to set up this new reality, they were ready to take to violent means wherever necessary.

During the Middle Ages, Christian and Muslim soldiers battled each other for centuries in the Crusades. The soldiers on both sides believed profoundly that they were the messengers of a new world. Towards the beginning of the twentieth century in India, particularly in the decade after the partition of Bengal in 1905, a number of small and big organisations remained busy in the attempt to end British rule through revolutionary means. Their aim was to create a new nation, which they dreamt would be a temple to Mother India. Whenever violent means are undertaken, there is an attempt to fundamentally change established systems and create a new order of reality. When exploitative governments use their power to suppress or torture opposing ideologies or persons, the violence of those in power also reflects an obstinate desire to perpetuate the reality of their making. Every act of violence has the purpose of asserting one's claim over a given establishment or to establish a new order. Regardless of the levels of serotonin in the brain, when individuals find themselves unable to change the world around them through accepted means and find it impossible to bear the agony of an existing order of reality, even ordinarily meek persons take recourse to violence. School and college-going youth casually pelt stones at their libraries and classrooms during agitations; parents beat their own offspring without the slightest awareness of their actions; while walking on the street, an already desperate person abuses and curses when he is accidentally jostled; these people feel that all avenues to construct a framework of the reality they wish to have are closed to them. Constructing a different reality, or at least asserting one's right to do so, is one of the impelling drives behind violent acts.

But it is precisely this force through which social reformers, thinkers, seers, and inspired artists perform their work. There is an intimate relationship between every creative act and every violent deed. Just as the creation of every god is accompanied by the creation of a corresponding demon, just as the gods have no significance without the demons, for any constructive worker to emerge, there is the need (according to Durkheim's theory, alluded to earlier) for people with violent tendencies.

If the motives behind violence are to create a new structure of reality, then violence will compare well with artistic creativity. The poet, the painter, the sculptor, and artists of every hue are troubled by established conventions of the world; they are in search of ways to change it. According to Sigmund Freud, the world of the artist is peopled with daydreams. Within the censorious regime of the social code, a creative way of channelling the individual's suppressed desires, perversities, and individuality comes through art. Freud thought that every work of literature clearly revealed the criss-crossing weave of the poet's desires, dreams, fears, frustrations, hate, and jealousy. Through the medium of words, colour, and rhythm, art attempts to make possible what is not possible in the actual and established reality. The reality of the art world is significantly different from ordinary everyday reality. Nevertheless, since both have similarities, art reality was termed 'virtual reality' by Susan Langer.[23] Such a virtual reality is sought to be created through violent acts as well. People who participate in violence have the satisfaction of at least momentarily changing reality.

Moreover, just as an artist feels invaded by an unseen force at the time of creating her/his work, a violent person may behave as if possessed at the time of committing violence. Great writers and painters create a new language, colour, or style in their work, which means that while a writer uses a known language such as English or Marathi, or a painter uses blue, red, and other known colours, the power of the language, its style and rhythm is something that will have never been expressed before. Within the confines of the available space on the canvas, the painter constructs a new world. Violent persons too create new and different kinds of relationships, other than those that society establishes as social relations. When the hands that normally join in a greeting are used to strangle the throat of the person before them, the attempt is to establish a new relationship that goes beyond expected social relations. The difference is that a writer creates this relation through language systems, the painter on the space on the canvas, while the violent person uses the medium of other peoples' bodies for this action. Violent individuals who use the medium of the body and actual physical reality in order to fulfil their dreams are perverse artists of a kind. If aesthetics had the tools to test the chemistry of creativity, perhaps anthropology would have found it possible to evolve its own tools to understand the chemistry of violence. Unfortunately, even in aesthetics, it has not been possible to gain a clear understanding of the creation of art. Therefore, the act of violence has remained—as are the divinely inspired arts—an eternal and unsolvable riddle in human life.

Ashis Nandy has made an insightful study of violence in the modern world.[24] According to him, the texture and quality of violence in the twentieth century are completely different from that in all earlier times. Whenever violence occurred in earlier times, there was an awareness that the killer and the killed were both human creatures. Whatever the degree of rage in the slayer and however inhuman his cruelty, the acts of violence were accompanied by the recognition that the slain could also be taken over by fury, that they too could be equally cruel. In other words, it was not denied that those who fell prey to violence were also human. But in the twentieth century, people are killed systematically and in cold blood. Just as a farmer sprinkles insecticides on his fields to wipe out germs and insects without the slightest anger—rather, he does so with a peaceful mind and a sense of duty—scientists, political leaders, soldiers, and police officials in the twentieth century are seen to annihilate groups holding opposite views with pride in their duty, without allowing human sympathies to disturb them emotionally. Ashis Nandy notes that in the past 100 years there has been genocide of nearly 110 million, entirely due to human volition. But merciless killing, done out of a feeling of duty or to implement law, leads to a dehumanisation of the killer. According to Nandy, an outstanding police officer may be able to control insurgencies, but in the process, the police officials in his department gradually, and unconsciously, acquire demonic tendencies.

In June 1994, the Supreme Court ordered the hearing of fifty-eight police officers of Uttar Pradesh. These officers had, in the previous year, arrested and later killed ten innocent youths on the allegation of being terrorists. The reality, however, was that they had no connection with terrorism in Punjab, and were on a pilgrimage to Huzoorsahib and other religious places in Maharashtra. The police captured them on a bus and killed them. Fortunately, the deaths of these youths became widely known, and the Supreme Court asked the guilty police officers for an explanation; unfortunately, however, in many other states of India and in many other countries, hundreds of people fall victim every day to similar police 'encounters'. Violence has almost become an industry during the twentieth century. The architects of political violence are able to manipulate the genocide of countless innocent people without getting a drop of blood on their hands. A political leader like Hitler could sit in his own private chamber and bring about the deaths of innumerable people. In the twentieth century, violence has come to be sold and bought by people like so many sanitised factory products, nicely wrapped in colourful paper.

In the twentieth century, violence has enveloped every aspect of human affairs. Just as human violence that manifests in words is different from the wordless violence of wild animals, the marketable violence of the twentieth century is different from the violence of the preceding centuries. It is possible to control, through medical means, the violence stemming from the defective production of chemicals in the brain, a diseased psychological state of mind, and the anger produced from a fear of impotence, but not, however, violence emerging from religion, nation, language, or race. The violence set in motion by a particular ideology can be countered by putting forward an opposing philosophy. The incidence of crime in society can be checked to an extent by undertaking programmes to eradicate poverty. But it is impossible to stop the marketable and inhuman violence of the twentieth century by these traditional solutions. To do so, it may be necessary to discover radically new routes of human progress. Until now, all studies on violence have placed the responsibility for violence on the individual, and the responsibility for such violent individuals on the inequality in society.

We might ask if violence emerges from the notion of progress that has been upheld for the past two or three centuries. Among the few visionaries who thought and spoke along these lines are Aurobindo Ghosh, Mahatma Gandhi, and J. Krishnamurti, all Indian thinkers. In 1909, Mahatma Gandhi in his short but radical book *Hind Swaraj* questioned the established goal of progress in the modern world. Today, over a century later, while thinking about the violence in our times, it is imperative that this question be raised once more. Among the issues raised by Gandhi, education, and the relation of progress with power and social morality are the most important. Although the context of violence has changed in our time, any attempt to understand the essential nature of violence must take a fresh look at these issues.

THE END OF INNOCENCE

If we believe that violence is caused by the procedures of socialising, then it becomes necessary to examine the system of raising children in a given society. The psychology of the members of any society is determined by the kind of schooling available to it. Today, children are required to attend school in most societies; it is considered a desirable practice. If we look at school children in India, we will notice that we may well be producing a generation of young people with broken backs. School weighs heavily on children in more ways than one. Such a generation may carry a psychological burden of violence throughout their lives. And this is but an outward symptom of a process submerged in the psyche of children. In ancient societies, knowledge was transferred from one generation to the next in an informal, non-institutionalised form. One did not have to go to formal schools in order to learn or get a document certifying learning. Today, if children do not go to schools, they are refused certificates confirming their education and rejected by society as useless. Jobs, economic advantages, and social acceptance evade them. In a sense, this certificate, an official stamp of education, has become a synonym for normalcy. In contemporary society, there is no room for children who do not want to attend school. Society today compels all children to be 'normal'; it is in the business of turning all children into normal children. And it may not make room for extraordinary children either. It may be practical to insist on uniformity in education and on certifying the normality of children, but it is not the most ideal way of educating them.

A related phenomenon in India is the dramatic increase in the number of schools. However, those who educate children are not necessarily competent to take care of young minds. The once noble profession of teaching has become, today in India, a nexus between greed and insensitivity. The teacher who has, in all probability, paid a hefty bribe for his recruitment attempts to recover this amount by providing tuitions. He has no other way and he cannot be blamed for this. Tuitions look for ways of providing incentives to attract students, and the incentive normally is the promise of easy success. The children who join the tuition classes are given slightly better marks than those who do not join them. It is a simple and practical transaction. The consequence is that the child learns from a very early age to purchase success. In the world outside the school, it is necessary to learn specialised skills to perform specialised jobs, which are generally in short supply. There is little room for all the degree holders in that competitive market of skilled labour, and this is underlined during adolescence when children come under stupendous pressure to succeed in that environment of scarce opportunity. Children who have had the experience of getting better results by paying for them will expect the same in the competitive market for employment. One immediate result is that they will enter the competitive world with a degree of cynicism and violence, rather than with a sense of confidence.

In larger towns, adolescent students very often give vent to their cynicism and violence by forming peer groups, which then, as a way of self-expression, begin to indulge in petty crime. Since there is a large number of such gangs in all the big towns of India, a general ethos of violence is forged. Violence as a social substance receives a certain tacit sanction. This ethos is reflected in all forms of dreams in Indian society. Cinema and television are the two most pervasive forms of such social dreams. The scale and degree of violence in Indian cinema is a result of the turmoil within the minds of the young.

The structure of violence in mainstream cinema is as follows. The main participant in that world of illusions has to undergo some acid tests in the form of violent physical engagements and emotional gestures. When he passes these tests, he is certified as the newborn hero. Becoming a hero in commercial cinema is based on his being violent; his new identity is a manifestation of the latent violence and cynicism. The process begins in school and concludes with the collective dream of our society.

Together with such dreams grows an attendant political ideology, which translates the dream world of violence into a programme for action. Political ideologies of hatred do not by themselves have the capacity to attract mass support, unless the masses have nurtured the emotion of hatred for long years. In India, there is a nexus between faulty education, the adolescent dreams that we dream collectively, and the politics of crime, which is the last and visible consequence of that larger alliance.

An important question that needs to be asked at this point is: How much knowledge do human beings really require? The answer will be that they require just enough knowledge to enable them to perform competently in their respective fields of activity. The present system of education loads the minds of children with huge quantities of excess information, far beyond their requirement. The cruel competition in the areas of employment and this heavy pressure to internalise knowledge may lead to a national genetic disorder. At no time in the past have we trained children in this manner; in no period of our history have we loaded the school bags and minds of our children with such an excess of knowledge. There was always space for leisure, space that has been rapidly shrinking. In its place, we instead find the dream world of violence, which occupies the imagination of the young generation. Even parents are sucked into the educational system as surrogate children. The system involves them in the child's admission interview, preparation for studies and exams, and in other activities. The educational system occupies much of the social space and privacy of homes. On the one hand, it reduces the period of childhood and on the other, it substantially increases the period for which a child is required to stay in the educational track. In the past, there was a correspondence between the biological and psychological periods of childhood and adolescence. With the years of education that a middle-class person receives today, the actual period of childhood is reduced drastically, while the period of education has increased substantially. Therefore, there is an unhealthy disagreement between the body and the social practice that children have to submit.

Obviously, something is wrong with this kind of education. Education is meant for the emotional and intellectual growth of children, yet it denies them their very childhood. In such a situation, neither emotion nor intellect can develop well. Instead, such education creates, in the mind of the child, a vacuum, and at the national level, a psychological disorder. India has the second largest population in the world, but its achievements in practically every area have been relatively poor. The responsibility must, in the final analysis, rest in the flawed education imparted to our children. If, as a nation, our collective dreams are frustrated in the international arena, they may give rise to extremely violent international conflicts. All Indian thinkers of significance during the twentieth century have tried to focus attention on this issue. Gandhi, Tagore, Aurobindo, and J. Krishnamurti have made serious attempts to understand the discordance between human nature and the knowledge cultivated in schools. The nation, however, has failed to take their warnings with sufficient seriousness. In the manner of Blake, one can ask today, 'Is it a holy thing to see, so many children tortured in school?'

During the past two centuries, the aesthetics in India have perhaps been the aesthetics of conflict. The model of education established by British colonial rule, post Macaulay, to basically train Indians for employment in the British government, is the model that has been followed by independent India these past seventy years. A second model of education, which hoped to address the spiritual and creative potential in the child, was evolved by visionaries like Tagore, Aurobindo, and Krishnamurti. Throughout the history of independent India, these two models have worked at cross purposes. This conflict is at the core of our vision of education in this country. The attempt to make children 'normal' by straitjacketing them in the first model sanctions no space to be oneself as advocated in the second model. It does not result in the maximum fulfillment of potential, which was the aim set out by many Indian thinkers of the twentieth century. Our poverty today in the fields of philosophy and social thought has lowered the guard against the tendency towards violence that the education system generates.

If the West, through capitalism and industrialisation, has hurt the natural resources, we in India have ill-treated and harmed our human resources. There is no term yet to describe the destruction of childhood in the name of education in this country. In the West, education has produced knowledge which encourages the exploitation of nature; in India, we have produced an educational system that results in violence. Although huge resources are expended in funding education, India has perhaps only managed to convert creativity into violence; all it has managed to create is to fuel the spiralling machinery of violence.

In this connection, the Vora Committee Report deserves to be read as a serious warning to the nation. It is an in-depth study of the dynamics of crime and its close link with politics. The brief of this Committee was to investigate the nature of violence in the country. The investigation revealed a fairly repetitive pattern of violence, beginning with the small-town school dropout forming a gang engaged in small-time crime. This gang then graduates to buying police protection for larger offences, such as smuggling and drug trafficking. At this stage, the gang leader may buy political patronage and become an extension of the political network. Gradually, he gravitates towards active politics. From this legally established position, he is free to facilitate the smooth functioning of his criminal activities and the further infiltration of criminals into decision-making positions. It would not be wrong, therefore, to infer that the raw material for political decision-making is drawn from the unruly edges of the violent school system.

THE MASCULINE STATE

It is necessary to think about the kind of State that India has visualised, accepted, and perpetuated in order to understand the nature of violence in our time. During the Indian freedom movement, the Indian National Congress gave shape to the dream of independent India as a strong and united nation, united in spite of its amazing diversity, which would be a shining example to the rest of the world. This goal of the freedom struggle of a reconstructed, united India took its inspiration from the philosophy of nationalism that European political history had generated. The Congress also accepted the model of British parliamentary democracy to govern the federation of such a large variety of traditional administrative units. It is important to understand that in his *Hind Swaraj*, among many other issues pertaining to the future of India, Gandhi discusses the question of the parliamentary form of government for India. This book presents his thought in the form of a dialogue with Indian revolutionaries. Gandhi's argument is that driving the British out of India by itself changes nothing if India is to merely replicate Britain in administrative matters. Shocking his contemporary society, Gandhi said in no uncertain terms that Parliament was like a prostitute, a statement that he refused to change even thirty years later when the book was going in for a reprint. He justified his epithet by reasoning that the elected representatives of Parliament are encouraged by the nature of the very system; they never do any good for its own sake and only do what the people want them to—that is, not the right things, but things that please. Parliament depends on the mercy and the pleasure of the people. Nor does it transact any useful business. Gandhi further pointed out that the Members of Parliament hardly attend sessions unless the Whip directs them to do so. Even when there is attendance, it is more often than not unruly, or the members attend only to claim privileges. This is not an argument against democracy; rather, it is a caution against thinking of parliamentary government as the essence of democracy.

After accepting democracy and the parliamentary form of government, independent India created a federation of Indian states, on the pattern of the United States of America, by merging all erstwhile princely states. Diverse cultures, communities, and language groups were brought into the federation. Further, it was accepted that India as a nation had to have armed forces to defend it; and since it was surrounded by some hostile nations, it had to have well-maintained armed forces. Parliament has final control over the army, the navy, the air force, the police, and the paramilitary forces. It thus becomes the law-enforcing agency, and a very powerful one. Political power supported by an army and a police force can only be masculine. The preparedness of the armed forces is also seen as a mechanism for stabilising external relations with other countries.

Most citizens today want to be close to the Parliament, the seat of power. Even if becoming a minister or Member of Parliament is out of one's reach, a desired ambition is to climb up the ladder of power, which gravitates towards the Parliament. The process may not be immediately visible, but when a small segment of any activity in national life is examined, it immediately becomes clear that schools, panchayats, corporate bodies, all aspire towards getting closer to the centre of this masculine political power. In this country, most of us live in a dream world crowded by metaphors of power; we secretly desire to be a presence in the power structure. In a sense, a majority of Indians aspire to wear the mask of masculinity. Since all power in this country is mistakenly seen as emanating from Parliament, and since Parliament is formed in the image of man, all of us have accepted the mask of masculinity as a desirable identity marker.

In this process, we are losing an extremely significant and valuable part of our cultural personality. The diverse cultures of India, which have over these many centuries evolved the delicate and the humane, the feminine part of the national personality, are in grave danger of losing their selfhood. This is the second source of violence in the Indian psyche. We have created a powerful centre of authority, which is sucking all of us into its masculinity, taking us away from our femininity, taking away from us our real federal structure. Perhaps the kind of change taking place in the personality of India would not have occurred had India not accepted the parliamentary system of government and if India had not become a nation-state. Had we retained our status of many 'nations', there would perhaps have been no shift to this all-male identity. Indian culture is a culture of diversity. It is a culture of heterogeneity. But the nature of the State in India is not in agreement with the nature of Indian culture.

If the scale of violence has gone up in India after Independence, there must be some correspondence between the nature of the State that we have created and the incidence of violence. We have become parts of a political machine, which has created an imbalance of personality within us, of which we are perhaps unaware. There is a need to create an alternative political system, and therefore there is a need to rethink what Gandhi had said about the Parliament. We must think of *swaraj*, rather than the *raj*. *Swara*j is self-discipline and for self-discipline, one must be in a profound communion with one's own self. What we have tried to create in India is a large-scale copy of any Western nation. We must now try to be India. Gandhi's alternative to parliamentary democracy was governance by people in small communities without a powerful centre. He advocated the principle of local self-government, which provides for minute regional variations within the general framework of a national democracy.

The aspiration to enter the power circle and the resolve to make India a nation have compelled us to homogenise the widely different ways of life and cultures. In the process, we have lost our varied cultural personalities. The system of governance after Independence does not agree with our cultural *prakruti* or selfhood. A fallout of this phenomenon is that as soon as any government is elected to power, a sense of disillusionment sets in. Due to the clash between our desire for a government that we need and the government that we elect, tremendous pent-up violence is built into our psyche, which surfaces at the slightest provocation. It is not enough to think of just riots, assassinations, and insurgencies. It is not enough to think about the import of arsenal from Sweden or France. It is not enough to think about atrocities on adivasis and nomads, or gender discrimination. Although all these are real manifestations of violence, what is more real is what we are doing to children in schools and the kind of government we have accepted.

If India is to tackle the problem of violence at its roots, then it is necessary to re-think the form of State that we have chosen. It is then that India can dream of a society free from violence. However, this change cannot be brought about through violence. All violent revolutions, which begin with the idea of changing the State, always end in greater violence. Violence produces nothing but counter-violence. Therefore, pacifist ways of changing the present form of State will have to be invented. One way to do so is to encourage femininity, which is opposed to the kind of State that we have today. It can be drawn from the source of Indian traditions. Femininity is devotion, love, and art. The present State encourages a parallel set of values, such as craftiness, and not craft. It does not encourage love, it encourages hatred. It divides us as Hindu against Muslim, rich against poor, upper caste against lower caste, rural against urban. And instead of devotion, the State encourages a selfish loyalty to power. Devotion does not admit greed, but the State encourages attachment to power. We have to choose between these two sets of values: loyalty, hatred and craftiness, or devotion, love and art. This choice is the most necessary political statement against violence that an ordinary Indian citizen can make.

Social Structure

Another important factor contributing to violence is the social structure in India. I have had the opportunity to speak with a number of men convicted of burning their wives. One of them had secured an MA in English Literature and happened to be a former student of the university where I used to teach. Another was a schoolteacher from north Gujarat. A third hailed from Bulsar in southern Gujarat. I met them on a number of occasions and spoke to them at length.

They were all very young, and I could not imagine them killing their wives. The one from Bulsar had failed his matriculation exam and had started working as a salesman in a pharmaceutical company, after having furnished a fake certificate. He lost his job when he was found out, after which he asked his father-in-law for some capital to start a business of his own. His father-in-law refused and this young man, with the help of his mother, burned his wife so that he could marry again for dowry. His father-in-law went to the police and this man was sentenced to rigorous life imprisonment. In India, a life sentence does not mean the entire life, but only fourteen years, which can be further reduced on the condition of good behaviour. He killed his wife when he was twenty-three; when he comes out of jail at the age of thirty-two or so, his family and society will accept him and take him back. In fact, his mother, also without remorse, has already arranged for a second marriage. He was in no doubt that he would be accepted, since his justification was that he had committed the crime on his parents' advice. He was doing it for his parents, it was his duty, and the responsibility was not his. It was, for him, a sacrifice.

The schoolteacher's wife was not very well-educated. It appeared that there was a female student in his school, with whom he became a little too friendly. His defence was that the girl was interested in studies and he was encouraging that interest. His wife objected to this friendship. At this, the teacher took a wood block and hit his wife with it. Even after she fell down, he continued hitting her with the block till her head was crushed to a pulp. Her parents lodged a complaint with the police when the village was preparing for the funeral. He too was awarded a fourteen-year term. When I asked the schoolteacher to name his favourite person in the world, he said it was Mahatma Gandhi, 'because Gandhi had never told a lie'. He said that he had never lied in his life. He had confessed his actions immediately to the policemen. He quoted from the Ramayana and, comparing himself with Rama, said there was a long tradition that sanctioned the kind of act he had committed.

There are a number of such cases, and these provide us with sufficient material to describe the structure of violence involved in the practice of wife-killing in India. In the first case, the parents seem to have accepted the killing of a young bride as a perfectly normal social practice. In the second case, the murderer justifies his deed as sanctioned by cultural practice. This is a reflection of the confused state of moral and social values in India today. A large majority of Indians live in an ethos in which crime can be excused if it conforms to certain accepted social and moral norms.

Simultaneously, the modern capitalist economy has created new material desires in the psyche of individuals. In fact, the individual is almost defined in terms of desires and not spiritual attributes. The market celebrates the freedom to desire and the need to succeed. The huge machinery of media, entertainment, and advertisement grounds every human emotion in the world of material things. Most emotions seem to culminate in the desire for success in work or erotic love. The individual is thus a victim of this network of desires, especially erotic desire. Most criminals in our society are victims of the huge market of desires. Within it, all human actions have lost their significance, except in terms of gratification of the senses. The general atmosphere of greed and craving for material success encourages a culture of violence. An already oppressive social system has become unbearably exploitative; and within this system, there is unprecedented violence against women and children.

Similarly, the instances of violence against the oppressed castes, the dalits, and the economically disadvantaged have increased over the past few decades. The Bhagalpur blinding of 1980 and the killing of tribals in a rally at Nagpur in 1994 are some of the better-known instances. All available statistics show that atrocities are rampant in India. There is clearly a link between the crimes committed by individuals and the violence caused by social groups. At the basis of both is the desire for material possession and wealth, which drives our collective minds, again on an unprecedented scale. Never before in the history of India had desire become so central to the social order. Material wealth is sought to acquire 'a new body' (as discussed earlier in connection with cinema) which is resistant to violence, which transcends violence. It is a body hungry to consume all the pleasures sold in the market of desires. The desires sold as commodities have in fact turned violence, too, into a commodity, which in a way helps in the acquisition of the other commodities. In short, there is a nexus between violence and desire, which is even more fearful than the nexus between crime and politics. The traditional social structure, with its history of caste, tribal, and gender discrimination, creates an already available space for the circulation of desire as violence. Violence is the inevitable mediator in the social conflicts that traditionally existed in Indian culture. Contemporary society is a terrifying social scenario: a result of the rapid breakdown of dialogue between the upper caste and dalit, the adivasi and non-adivasi, the rich and the poor, the urban and the rural. India appears to have become an extremely violent country ready for an unprecedented scale of violence, generated from within the institutions of knowledge, the political structure, and social inequality.

COUNTERING VIOLENCE

The aim of legal systems is to deter violence by punishing those who transgress the law. But it is always difficult to decide whether a person acts violently because he has no respect for the law, or because he is not in full control of his faculties. That is, it is difficult to determine if violence emerges from a psychic disorder or deviation from a given social norm. Is it subversion of established practice or perversion in the human mind? The legal system only classifies the cases of individual violence in an arbitrary manner. The legal way of understanding violence is guided by its classification in terms of arson and looting, suicide and murder, assault and crime, war, acts of insanity, and so on. This, it must be admitted, is somewhat crude. Since we do not understand violence, we have been unable to come to terms with it and to counter it. There have been occasional efforts to address the entire phenomenon by individuals like Jesus Christ and Mahatma Gandhi; but these have not sunk into the collective psyche of humanity. Gandhi interpreted violence as essentially a result of greed, both in an individual life and in the public domain. He proposed that freedom from desire is non-violence, not only in terms of acts of violence, but also with regard to concepts and feelings. That is, violence is manifest in deeds, but perhaps more importantly, it lies deep within thoughts. He considered it a phenomenon residing in the human mind and interpreted violence as an excess of masculine qualities.

In *Intimate Enemy*, Ashis Nandy analyses Gandhi's opposition to British colonial masculinity by privileging femininity. Passive resistance, *satyagraha*, non-cooperation were all Gandhi's weapons to fight the aggressive British rule. His entire struggle against colonial rule took the form of a struggle of '*stritva*' against the British '*purushatva*'. But purely academic efforts to understand violence do not go very far in reducing it. It is one thing to understand that violence arises out of desire, but quite another to create a society free of desire. For the past three centuries, human history has been a gigantic story of the creation of desire. Ever since the great philosophers of Enlightenment such as Galileo, Kepler, and

Copernicus made scientific discoveries in astronomy, the human being has come to be the centre of the universe. The right to exploit natural resources for the material progress of human beings came to be taken for granted during this period. Increasingly sophisticated machines that reduce labour and produce commodities that gratify desire have been created, in the process reducing the dignity of labour and enhancing desire. To have more and to have the ability to have more are considered indications of human progress. This ideology is concurrent with a certain moral framework that is indifferent to the needs of the ecology. Industrialisation has rarely cared for the well-being of nature; industrial society likes to imagine nature as a mute entity, without intellect or language.

In a sense, the history of the past three centuries has been a tyranny of speech over silence: it is a history of the self-obsessed language of oppression. The social space that used to be occupied by silence has been erased. At present, progress is measured in terms of the ability to produce more, to possess more, and to consume more than we really need. This is the new ethic, the new *dharma.* The rhetoric of modernity and the ideology of progress boils down to what Gandhi called violence. No world organisation ever attempts to persuade people to improve their conscience. The ones that teach thus have become obsolete and irrelevant. The entire ethos is engaged in building a world of desires. Those who oppose this, such as the church and other religious organisations, are today seen as redundant. This is because they still invoke the idea of God in the name of good. It is difficult to believe that God exists in any form of existence that we can know. The medieval saint-poet Kabir knew this; he had no hesitation in stating that whoever created the fish also created the net that caught it. The existence of a supreme power, God, was not to be taken as an absolute *a priori* proposition. The human teacher, guru, was probably more immediate as well as of a greater significance. If God was a mere maker of existence, the person with knowledge was the one who understood it, the one who had knowledge about it. Perhaps we need to revive Kabir's understanding of God as a passive agency if we have to release ourselves from the trap set by fundamentalist religious groups.

In the space vacated by religion, secular institutions like the World Trade Organization (WTO), World Health Organization (WHO), World Bank, etc., have stepped in and made it their business to spread the message of material acquisition. The failure of the past three centuries has been the failure to create a non-theological, but yet spiritual force counter to the ideology of industrialisation and material advancement.

As the most important thinker to counter the materialism inherent in modernism, Gandhi attempted to combine politics with religion in order to create spiritual buffers. Because the ethical framework surrounding technological civilisation is unquestioned, violence remains the order of the day. Nature and people who are termed 'primitive' are routinely destroyed so as to gratify multiplying desires. Modern civilisation is based on unrestricted violence. Of course, there have been a few attempts to change this situation: Communism, for instance, was one such attempt. However, it tried to control the greed of individuals without removing the source of it. It failed to understand that the solution to violence is not counter-violence. Gandhi's method for countering violence was non-violence.

It may be interesting to examine this position closely. Implicit in non-violence is a certain degree of passivity. No defence of non-violence can rule this element out. Gandhi, one must not forget, also stated that the violence of a courageous person is preferable to the non-violence of a coward. I should like to argue that the true alternative to violence is not non-violence, but a dynamic constructive activity. The constructive action should be for our time and our society, and not just an imitation of what great minds have done in the past.

When we think of the opposition between violence and non-violence, the Gita necessarily comes to one's mind. It is a text that emerged from an intense moment of violence; it is a poem in the form of advice for action. In India, there are these two counter-points when we think of violence: Gandhi, who preferred non-violence to action, and the Gita, which advocates violence, rather than non-action.

The Gita became a crucially important text at the beginning of the twentieth century when India was evolving a new political identity for herself. A number of philosopher-leaders worked on it—Sri Aurobindo wrote *Essays on the Gita,* Tilak composed *Gitarahasya*, Gandhi translated the Gita and also wrote a series of letters commenting on his translation. These three interpretations of the Gita are important because the three thinkers were among the makers of the destiny of modern India. The interpretations emerge from a very deep contemplation of the political activity that they were involved in.

Tilak's essays have to be located in the context of a tradition of philosophy that dates back to the thirteenth century, a tradition that originates in Jnanadev's commentary on the Gita. These essays offer reflections on the long continuing debate on whether the Gita teaches action, *pravrutti,* or detachment, *nivrutti.* The debate has focused on the concept of a *sthitapragnya*: a person who retains his equanimity in the midst of turmoil and suffering. The second chapter of the Gita discusses the detached person, the *sthitapragnya*, in elaborate detail. Krishna charts the daily routine of such a person as also the quality of his inner world, and sets out the oft-quoted comparison with the lotus blooming in a muddy pond. This leads Krishna to the definition of the soul: it does not get drenched in water, does not burn when set afire, nor dries in the wind; the definition rests on its description of detachment. This has led to a philosophical debate around the opposition between action and inaction. The

Gita states that desire attached to action leads to sorrow; and so, before Tilak's time, the Gita had often been interpreted as a text advocating passivity. Tilak's persuasive argument was that above everything else, the Gita teaches a sense of responsibility towards the action expected of man, and failure to act amounts to failing in his duty. His interpretation of the Gita foregrounds the *karmamarga.*

Sri Aurobindo offers a substantially different interpretation of the Gita, although there is little doubt that his essays were inspired by Tilak's interpretation. Tilak and Aurobindo were contemporaries and had worked together for a while in the Indian National Congress. Aurobindo understands the Gita to be knowledge, *jnana.* He himself had formulated a philosophy of evolution from matter to mind, and from the mind to the super mind. In his opinion, the Gita points to this theory of this evolutionary process. He focused on the Gita's interpretation of the Sankhya school of philosophy, characterised by its discussion of a cyclical progress from *tamasa* to *sattva.* His reading was that the Gita unfolds an image of the world known through the medium of thought. Therefore, his discussion of the text privileges knowledge over both devotion and action. As active contemporaries in national politics, Tilak and Aurobindo's understanding of the Gita was not just a philosophical exercise. Their ultimate objective was freedom for the millions of Indians and understanding of the Gita was a means of seeking that freedom. Their attempt was to make the Gita relevant to modern India.

Gandhi entered the national political scene in India soon after Tilak and Sri Aurobindo had reached their political pinnacle. His interpretation of the Gita is particularly interesting, given his views on violence. Gandhi's translation of the Gita was probably not much appreciated, and his followers raised some questions about his interpretative translation. In order to defend it, he wrote seven letters, which were published independently. The first of these letters persuades the reader to begin reading the translation from the fifth chapter of the Gita, which views Arjuna as a *bhakta.* Thus, for him, the Gita is mostly about devotion, love, and compassion. Gandhi wished to focus on the fact that although Krishna speaks of war and action, Arjuna is primarily a devotee, and an undue emphasis on action in war is to misinterpret the Gita. Krishna himself stresses on *bhakti* when he says that knowledge and action without devotion are not of much value. Thus, Gandhi claimed that devotion is the essence of the Gita.

The Gita is essentially a poem; it is to be understood as a philosophy only after it is recognised as a poem, and hence, open to several readings. The above discussion highlights its different interpretations as *karmamarga*, *jnanamarga*, and *bhaktimarga*: from the three great nationalists who shaped the destiny of India during the twentieth century. If one can think of the history of India as an unfinished, still to be resolved story, and of Tilak, Aurobindo, and Gandhi as characters in this story, one can perhaps look at the question of violence from a fresh perspective.

The history of India in the early part of the twentieth century was dominated by the philosophy of non-violence. At the same time, it has been a history that is tremendously interested in the question of violence as discussed in the Gita. If the story has to be brought to some conclusion, how shall we face the question of violence again? The conclusion can only be this: that non-violence is not the opposite of violence. Its opposite is constructive action. We must also realise that to read the Gita in terms of action alone, or knowledge alone, or only devotion, is not to understand it in its entirety. One hesitates to say this, for those three leaders emphasising *karmamarga*, *jnanamarga*, or *bhaktimarga* were without doubt great thinkers. It is perhaps more appropriate to understand the Gita as an integration of all the three. And with this understanding, if we invite Lord Krishna and Mahatma Gandhi into a dialogue once again in our presence, we will perhaps know why it is necessary to think of action of a certain kind as the countering force to violence.

Today, the significance of *jnanamarga* lies not in seeking knowledge about God alone, but in seeking to reform, and radically reform, the institutions of knowledge. This means that to put the Gita into practice, *jnanamarga* would involve making our educational system more responsible and more humane. *Bhaktimarga* today lies in rethinking the network of loyalties, *bhakti*, in which we are bound. It does not mean thinking only of devotion to God: that path has not succeeded in producing an alternative to technological civilisation. Today, there is a network of *bhakti* among the institutions that pervade our lives, with the State at its apex and all routes of devotion leading to that apex. The modern form of devotion has substituted God with the political State. It is important to rethink the nature of this *bhakti* to the State. Perhaps we need to look at small communities, at commitment to the local as against the pan-national or global. *Karmamarga* today would mean restructuring political ethics in our collective life to improve society to the best of one's ability, and not just accumulating spiritual virtue in an individual fashion.

If *bhakti, jnana*, and *karma* can be integrated in these forms, the task that the generation of Tilak, Aurobindo, and Gandhi began, and which we need to take to its fruition, will perhaps be completed. We may be able to evolve a viable alternative to violence in the form of constructive action through such integration. We must learn to look at Krishna as a statesman, not an avatar, and see the Gita as talking about man and not God. We need to combine Gandhi without his passive 'non-violence' but active 'constructive action' together with the Gita without its God. It is then that one might understand the core of violence in modern Indian society and be able to counter it. This will be the true antithesis of violence that has enveloped us so pervasively.

NOTES AND REFERENCES

1. Edwin H. Sutherland and Donald R. Cressey, *Criminology* (Philadelphia: J. B. Lippincott Company, 1970), 3. See also Edwin Sutherland and Donald R. Cressey, 'Differential Association Theory', in Delos H. Kelly (ed.), *Deviant Behavior: Readings in the Sociology of Deviance* (New York: St. Martin's Press, 1979), 93–99.

2. Hans J. Eysenck and Leon Kamin, *Intelligence: The Battle of the Mind* (London: Macmillan, 1981).

3. Karl A. Menninger, *The Crime of Punishment* (New York: Penguin Books, 1978).

4. *The New Scientist,* February 1994, 33.

5. Hannah Arendt, 'On Violence', in *Crises of the Republic* (San Diego: Harcourt Brace & Co., 1969), and 'Antisemitism', in *The Origins of Totalitarianism,* Part I (San Diego: Harcourt Brace & Co., 1972).

6. Robert Merton, 'Social Structure and Anomie', *American Sociological Review* Ill, reprinted in Delos H. Kelly (ed.), *Deviant Behavior* (New York: St. Martin's Press, 1979), 110–21. (This quote taken from p. 117.)

7. Emile Durkheim, *The Rules of Sociological Method,* Sarah A. Solovay and John H. Mueller (trans.) and George E. C. Catlin (ed.) (New York: The Free Press, 1938). Reprinted in Delos H. Kelly (ed.), *Deviant Behaviour,* 51.

8. Ibid., 53.

9. Ibid., 54.

10. Entry on 'Impotence', *Encyclopedia of Psychology* (London and New York: Continuum International Publication Group, 1972).

11. Adolf Hitler, *Mein Kampf* (Mumbai: Jaico Publishing House, 1988), 48.

12. Ibid., 152.

13. Ibid., 242.

14. In the original Marathi essay, Jnanadeva's celebrated translation of the Gita, the *Jnaneshwari*, is used. Here, the translation used is from the Ramakrishna Mission edition of the Gita, together with the commentary by Sankara and Swami Vivekananda. The translation used in some of the

subsequent passages draws on the Bhagavad Gita as rendered by Swami Gambhirananda (Calcutta: Advaitk Ashram, 2e, 1991).

15. *Bal Gangadhar Tilak, Srimad Bhagvadgita-Rahasya or Karma-Yoga-Sutra*, Bhalachandra Sitaram Sukthankar (trans.) (Pune: Gita Printers, 1935), xxviii.

16. Sri Aurobindo, 'The Creed of the Aryan Fighter', in *Essays on the Gita,* Sri Aurobindo Birth Centenary Library, 13, 1972, 58–59.

17. Ibid., 61.

18. Upendra Thakur, *The History of Suicide in India: An Introduction* (New Delhi: Munshiram Manoharlal, 1963), 61.

19. Ibid., 73.

20. Ibid., 77.

21. *The New Scientist,* February 1994.

22. Hans Torov, *Violent Men: An Inquiry into the Psychology of Violence* (Chicago: Aldine Publishing Co., 1969).

23. Susanne Langer, *Feeling and Form: A Theory of the Arts* (Routledge and Kegan Paul, 1953).

24. Ashis Nandy (ed.), *Science, Hegemony and Violence: A Requiem for Modernity* (Japan: The United Nations University, 1988, reprinted by Oxford University Press, New Delhi, 1990); 'The Discreet Charms of Indian Terrorism', in *The Savage Freud* (New Delhi: Oxford University Press, 1995), 1–31.

2
Kikiyario
Adivasi Voice and Violence

I

An extremely sharp exclamation, abrupt, entirely unexpected, prolonged, defiant, jubilant yet touched by pathos, an exclamation that is part animal, part human, and at its highest, a somewhat divine sound, a sound such as only tribals know how to articulate; such a sound, in Gujarati, is called a *kikiyari.* In the tribal oral traditions, it is never to be voiced in solo. It is to be used as a challenge to the companion in dance, as a collective approval in rituals, and as a war cry. This unscriptable cry is, therefore, always tribal and always in the plural, *kikiyario.* If tribals all over the world are divided a thousand times by clan, language, habitat, and nomenclature, they still remain united by the *kikiyario*, the most public expression of the most elemental substratum of their being.

I have heard the *kikiyario* in many different parts of India, and every time they have reminded me of William Blake: 'Is that trembling cry a song? Can it be a song of joy?' Each time, I have felt that there are centuries of silence between the tribals and us, and that they offer the *kikiyario* as a bridge for us to cross that vast silence. Many times I have been transposed to that other world of ecstasy and pain like a character in a Mahasweta Devi novel, or as Verrier Elwin or Shankar Guha Niyogi had been in their time.

My destiny is intertwined with that of the tribal village of Tejgadh.

II

Tejgadh is situated on the border of Gujarat and Madhya Pradesh, 90 kilometres east of Baroda. The name of the village seems to have been drawn from a hill nearby. The hill itself is now called Koraj Hill, but the relics of an eleventh-century settlement at the foot of the hill show a fortified area which was possibly the Tejgadh fort at one time. There is, however, no memory of this fort in the local folklore. The only basis for hazarding this guess is that the Koraj Hill is linked to the chain of hills that ends with Pavagadh, a pilgrimage place near the seat of the medieval capital of Gujarat, Champaner.

The population of Tejgadh and surrounding villages is predominantly tribal. These villages were ruled in the past by petty chieftains, and each of them built for himself a fortification in the Rajput style. Tejgadh may have been one of those kingdoms. However, the present village is situated 3 kilometres away from the Koraj Hill. The oldest settler family there can recall a history no older than 100 years. The family that claims to be the earliest to settle in Tejgadh is of the merchant class. However, the largest segment of the population is tribal, and their lifestyle is in continuity with the ancient and medieval tribal lifestyle of the region. Therefore, there is not enough to assume that Tejgadh had been in existence for centuries prior to the settling of the merchant families.

In terms of the village architecture, Tejgadh shows five layers of settlement. The earliest of these appears to have been the area of the village pond, near which lies a sixteenth-century step-well, which is no longer in use. The pond is approximately 400 metres away from the northern bank of the river Orsang. The next historical layer seems to be what is now known as Haridaspur, which is a cluster of about 170 tribal families. But most of these families carry on the traditional animistic practice of worship and have preserved their sacred groves. The third layer of habitation is at the foot of the Koraj Hill. However, the families settled there show no traces of lineage-relation with the historical Tejgadh fortification. They are all tribal families, and are clan relations of the families settled in Haridaspur. It is quite likely that they moved out of Haridaspur, subsequent to the decline of Tejgadh's political power, and claimed the land there for agricultural use. The fourth layer of settlement is the Limdi Falia, or the straw-market, around which the houses of the merchant class are built, and which are not older than 100 years. The last layer of settlement is the Rohit Falia, or the colony of low-caste Hindus, with houses built on the fringes of farms owned by the merchant class.

There are traces of three village ponds in Tejgadh. The oldest pond is closest to the river Orsang, and holds water even today. The second is close to the Rohitvas, about half a kilometre from the old pond; but it is now no more than a dry depression. A new road has been built to span it and it has been partially filled for that purpose. The third pond is near the Koraj Hill; it has completely dried up, but a view of the dry pond from the top of the hill shows how majestic it must have been at one time.

The river Orsang is a dry river with a sandy basin almost half a kilometre wide. It contains water only during the monsoon months, but turns into a trickle during the late winter months, when the river bed is used for watermelon cultivation. There is no temple in the river bed or along the banks of the river. On the whole, the Orsang does not enjoy much centrality in the emotional lives of the villagers in Tejgadh, nor does it enjoy a place of privilege in their festivals and rituals. Rather, it is seen as the line of natural defence.

There are no wells in Tejgadh that enjoy the status of community wells. Given that the tribals have their houses on their own farms, the existing wells are invariably agriculture-bound and used by individual families. There are about sixty such wells, with a mouth measuring a diameter of 20 feet on an average, and a depth of 80 feet.

The water supply for domestic use is arranged through pipelines. The village panchayat manages the Tejgadh waterworks. A tube-well has been dug for the purpose close to the panchayat building. Twelve hand pumps have been given to the village by the Taluka Development Office, spread evenly over different parts of the village.

The Tejgadh village can be seen as a chain of rings, each larger than the previous one. Thus, the innermost ring forms the habitation of the Hindu merchants. The next, slightly larger, is the habitation of Muslims and dalits. The next is the habitation of tribal families that have taken to vegetarian food habits and elements of Hindu marriage rituals, and who consider themselves '*sudharela*' (advanced/modern/reformed/gentry). The fourth ring, which is very large in scope, is the habitation of those tribals who still largely follow their ritual and social traditions. And the last ring, which covers an area of nearly 12 km in length, contains the isolated habitation of the poorest of tribals, who still survive on forest-gathering and farm labour. Of these, only the innermost ring, that is, the area where the Hindu merchant class resides, has a built drainage system. The gutters in Tejgadh are built with rubble- stone and are not covered. But most houses in the first two rings have latrines attached to them. The general practice is to build the latrine outside the main house, but within the compound area.

Three different places are used for cremation and burial—one for the Hindu merchants and dalits, the second for the Muslims, and the third for the tribals. All of them are at least a kilometre away from the village centre, that is, the Limdi Bazaar. There is only one place reserved for the disposal of dead animals, which is situated next to the railway track, since there are families that carry out the scavenging and skinning of dead animals. The disposal system is fairly efficient.

There are three public places of worship in Tejgadh. The most organised is the mosque, where prayers are offered punctually according to the customs of the Muslim families. There are two temples, one of which contains a Hindu deity of Mata or Laxmi, and the tribal hero Bhathuji. There is one temple in Haridaspur devoted exclusively to Bhathuji. However, there is a public meeting hall for the Vaishnavas, within which idols of Krishna are displayed and worshipped on special occasions. Near the Koraj Hill is a beautiful temple precinct; however, it is not in use now since the idols there are cracked. One can see relics of a Shiva temple and a broken *linga*.

The panchayat building is two-storied. The panchayat has also built other buildings, used for administrative work and for operating various government projects.

Tejgadh has a high school, an impressive and spacious building. It has three primary schools with fairly good structures, a primary health centre together with residential quarters for the medical staff, and a veterinary doctor's service station.

Tejgadh is connected by telephone to the rest of the world, and has a regular supply of electricity through a two-phase feeder. Therefore, television, radio, and microphones are used here. However, very few tribal families own television sets. The roads connecting Tejgadh with the taluka and district headquarters are of good quality, and the main mode of transportation outside the village is the diesel-driven automobile. And on all sides, it is surrounded by tribal villages.

III

When Gujarat was burning between 27 February and 4 March 2002, the tribal belt on the eastern border of Gujarat was quiet. The only exceptions were the two districts of Panchmahals, for which Godhra is the main town. Elsewhere in the tribal areas, tribals, Hindus, and Muslims continued to coexist peacefully. The only disturbing sight was the long lines of tribal labourers walking the distance from the curfew-bound cities to their villages, in some cases, a walk of 100 kilometres. They walked silently, carrying the burden of all their belongings on their heads, misery in their hearts, terrified like trapped animals.

Nearly 60,000 tribal labourers migrate to Baroda every year in search of employment between October and March. From the third day of the riots, these tribal labourers started returning to their villages. No public transport was available to them, so they decided to walk back like refugees trying to escape a devastated country.

The first Muslim shop to be set on fire in any tribal village was in Tejgadh. This case of arson took place on the evening of 4 March. During the night, two more shops were torched. The rural branch of the Baroda district police had not expected any reaction to the Godhra incident to come this late. On Tuesday, Senior DSP Keshav Kumar (who has prepared the first ever book on the Indian Penal Code, the IPC, in a tribal language for distribution amongst tribals) asked me to join him in his efforts to restore peace. When we arrived at Tejgadh, we saw a cloth shop being looted and set on fire by a mob. The DSP instantly fired tear-gas shells and dispersed the mob. From there, he proceeded to Chhota Udepur. Few had expected five army trucks to arrive in the area for night patrolling.

That night, no army personnel were present in Tejgadh. More shops, more houses were burnt in the village. Tejgadh has a miniscule Muslim population: 75 per cent are tribals, 15 per cent are Hindus, and 5 per cent are Muslims. Those who burnt the shops and houses came from the neighbouring villages, and in the initial stage, were quite drunk. But once the first attack was over, the other villagers joined in on their own with no further need for instigation, and the looting continued.

The incidents in Tejgadh displayed a method as well as a sequential growth in the theme of the disturbance. In the cities, at least for the first three days, the riots had the clear stamp of a well-researched and well-orchestrated strike. The attacks were marked with amazing precision. As against this, the villages in Panchmahals, Kheda, and Baroda districts displayed a blind anger. The incidents at Tejgadh were different from both; it was clear that they were not included in the master plan of violence, nor were the incidents unfolding in Tejgadh a frenzied reaction to the Godhra outrage.

The Muslim population in Tejgadh continued to stay in the village, carrying out their daily work with no apprehension of intimidation. On that day, Muslims in some other village were reportedly threatened by the local population; and it was initially maintained that all Muslims of Tejgadh had gone over to that village to defend those Muslims. It was said that the residents of Tejgadh were angered by this aggressive attitude on the part of the Tejgadh Muslims. As a result, one Muslim shop was set ablaze in Tejgadh on the evening of 4 March. It is said that Sarpanch Krishnakant Shah had tried to prevent those who wanted to start the arson, but was forced to give up in the face of their pressure and threats; it is also said that the arsonists came from outside. After the incident, no one in Tejgadh was prepared to name the arsonists. And nobody was able to say why all the Muslims had gone over to another village, and why not even one of them returned to Tejgadh to save the shops, houses, and vehicles that were burnt in regularly-tuned phases. No one was prepared to say how so much kerosene became available, and who led the mobs. And no one said why only properties belonging to Muslims were set on fire.

The Tejgadh carnage was leisurely; every day, one or two shops were burnt. In the very first instance, the mob was collected from the Timla, Koraj, and Achhala segments of the panchayat, all at a distance of 1–2 kilometres from Limdi Bazaar, the centre of the riots. In the second and third instances, the distance increased. Tribals from neighbouring villages wanted their share of the booty. The residents of Tejgadh had shut the doors of their houses and, in a self-imposed curfew, locked themselves in. When officially the curfew was imposed, it was only a formality.

The police force provided to watch the village was meagre, and after dispersing two or three rounds of mob attacks, it fell into the same conspiracy of inaction that the villagers had already hatched. Thus, on the twelfth day of the Tejgadh riots, yet another house was burnt, with neither the villagers nor the police ready to intervene and avert the action. On the thirteenth and fourteenth days, one or two more houses were burnt down. The ritual continued. If the violence in the cities stood out by its precision and in other rural areas by its blind frenzy, the violence in Tejgadh stood out by its ritual quality. It showed a cold-bloodedness in slow-time. This ritual quality was a clear indication that at this end of Gujarat, the theme of communalism was taking a back seat and had been taken over by the norms of tribal culture.

Therefore, when trouble began in Panvad, two days later and at a distance of 30 kilometres from Tejgadh, the stage was already set for a tribal takeover of the riots. Those with an interest in fanning the trouble had already started planting rumours that would provoke the tribals. Among the rumours that I heard, the following five deserve mention.

1. A tribal dreamt that a majestic mahuda, the most sacred tree of the Rathwas, had been chopped and used to block the road. Babadev, or the Babo Pithora God, was very angry and asked for revenge on those who had harmed the mahuda.
2. The police have come to believe that tribals have a mantra with which they can spellbind the police rifles; and therefore policemen are scared to use their weapons.
3. A certain Badwa, a shaman, has received divine inspiration to become the biggest Badwa, although he is only twenty-two years old. He has learnt all aspects of magic and cannot be killed. He will lead the tribals.

4. Muslims have been raping tribal women and kidnapping tribal girls and selling them in the cities.
5. Muslims have started taking away 'Kashmir' (a place or a girl) by exploiting tribals, and they have kept fifty tribal women locked up.

The location of Panvad is unique. Almost twenty small and big villages can be reached from this area in a very short time by walking cross-country. A number of Hindu sectarian movements have been active in the area for several years. Some Jain monks, probably from Rajasthan or Madhya Pradesh, have been living in a nearby village called Kawara, and wield considerable influence on the people. The Muslim businessmen in Panwad are considerably affluent. Most of them are engaged in moneylending at an interest rate ranging between 60–120 per cent.

Whether because of hatred for the moneylenders, or because of the rumours concerning the magical impediments to police ability, the congregation of tribals at Panwad was alarmingly large. According to newspaper reports, their numbers went up to 5,000. But considering that every village had sent about fifty to 100 people, the number of those who actually participated in the looting was a little less than 2,000 at any given time.

The ritual quality introduced by the Tejgadh events was in evidence on a magnified scale in Panvad. This time, the tribals were carrying their ceremonial bows and arrows with them. Normally, they never use arrows as weapons. When they want to kill someone, they use the sharp metallic *paliyu* or *dhariyu*; and when they want to fight a thief or an enemy, they try to use guns. Many of them possess a license to keep guns, and some buy them in illegal supply from Madhya Pradesh, which is just a few kilometres away. Arrows are used only by children for hunting birds. (Very few birds are left in that area.)

The first mob that attacked Panvad in these riots carried bows and arrows as a ritual decoration. But when it realised that mere mantras could not stop the policemen from firing, the next wave on the following day seems to have brought along guns as well. Senior DSP Keshav Kumar, a courageous and conscientious officer, told me that he encountered tribals who stood before him and bared their chests, daring him to fire. Such was their faith in the power of the rumoured mantra.

I was in Baroda when I learnt from HQ Officer Parmar that there was much trouble in Panvad, that one tribal had died in police firing, and that the tribals had fired more than 100 rounds. This was very disturbing news. The history of tribals in western India shows that once such a mood sets in, it takes a long time for things to return to normal.

I was also worried because in my view, violence is not the way for tribal development. And the sole purpose of creating the Tribal Academy at Tejgadh was to teach tribals the ways of empowerment through constructive hard work.

I was in Tejgadh on 9 March, primarily to hand over a letter to the Administrator of Tribal Sub-plan in Chhota Udepur. This was the second Saturday of the month. This is normally a holiday, but some of the staff of the Tribal Sub-plan would be in the office to sort out the work that piles up as the financial year draws closer to its end in March. Saturday is the day of the weekly *haat* or market in Chhota Udepur. On this Saturday, however, there were no vendors in the *haat*, and no buyers. In the past 100 years, the *haat* has remained closed not more than five times. Villagers from nearly seventy villages go to the Udepur *haat.* They all knew on 9 March that something unusual had been happening. The Panvad rumours spread rapidly through the medium of silence that the absent *haat* provided.

Sunday, 10 March, brought news of further disturbance in the tribal areas. The trouble was spreading to other towns like Kawant and Chhota Udepur. Things became worse on 11 March.

Throughout the days of the riots, one could see trucks carrying petrol or kerosene making ritual trips to these towns. Obviously many mysterious elements had a part to play in the riots. But the forensic side of the riots was altogether neglected by the media, even *The Times of India*, which carried an article by Dipankar Gupta on 14 March on the topic, on its edit page. Similarly, the sociological aspect was largely overlooked. The Gujarati press, on the other hand, created an image of the tribals as a gang of looters. But somewhere, despite the desire to not understand and not analyse, the Gujarati press was closer to the truth of the matter. All the Gujarati newspapers described how the tribals were mounting attacks while letting out frightening *kikiyario.*

IV

The press kept asking me about the tribal situation and quoted me several times during the days of the riots. *The Indian Express* reporter Swati Majumdar travelled with me to Tejgadh on 7 March to interview the residents there. However, she drew a blank as no one was prepared to risk making a statement. I continued to offer an analysis of the economic situation of the tribals till 13 March. On that day, District Magistrate Bhagyesh Jha and senior DSP Keshav Kumar were fired at by a tribal using a country gun. I thought then that I did not know enough about the situation and decided to keep quiet thereafter. It was on the same day that Jnanapith and Magsaysay award winner Mahasweta Devi wanted me to send a report for the Kolkata-based *Aaj Kaal.* I wrote the following:

> Riots spread to Panvad four days later and to Kawant seven days after they had erupted in Tejgadh. In Panvad the police had to resort to firing hundred and ten rounds on a single day; and the tribals who had been emboldened by then fired on police in return. The riots are still continuing and when they are brought under control in one village, another village goes up in flames.
>
> Everybody has been asking why tribals, who do not have any sympathy with Hindu fundamentalism, have got involved in the riots?

To explain this, I wrote about the socio-economic situation of the tribals:

> ... the literacy among women is less than 20 per cent, the rate of interest for loans from money lenders ranges between 60 to 120 per cent. Nearly 30 per cent population is carrier of sickle cell anaemia and three per cent of them confirmed sicklers. Medical facilities are inadequate and for the last three years the area has gone through a severe drought. Whoever initiated the riots ... will create a long term problem of tribal insurgency.
>
> What they [the tribals] need and want is a decent education, health and employment and not temples and religious leaders.

Throughout the day on 19 March, I had heard that it was almost certain that Chhota Udepur, which had remained tense but free from violence, would go the same way as Kawant, Panvad, and Bodeli. By that evening, some arrests had been made; and it appeared that the ring-leaders had been arrested. The fifteen-day tribal riots in Chhota Udepur taluka were over. No house or shop was burnt on 19 March in Tejgadh, Panvad, or Bodeli. By the morning of 20 March, the tone had changed. There was panic among the tribals. Their concern now was how not to get arrested.

However, the peace that appeared certain on 20 March turned out to be a mirage when, three days later, three more structures were set on fire in Tejgadh. Bodeli too remained smouldering; and of all places, Chhota Udepur, which had remained calm during the previous three weeks, started looking tense. Curfew had to be imposed there in the fourth week since the riots began. The fire lit in the tribal region was showing no signs of dying.

From the perspective of the tribals, it is necessary to raise some questions about the riots: Did the tribal population of Chhota Udepur region have any plans to rise up in a revolt? Was there any explicit or latent movement in the area bordering on a militant opposition to the state? Had the communal state government made such inroads into tribal life that the spirit of Hindutva had overtaken the local tribal culture? In other words, how much of the Muslim persecution in the tribal regions of Gujarat during the riots of March 2002 was *tribal* in character, and how much of it was a measure of political success? Answers to these questions are important, to understand the riots as well as the tribal situation.

One aspect of the entire episode that stood out from the very beginning of the riots was that the persecution of Muslims in Tejgadh and Panvad had not been spontaneous, or even as planned by the Sangh Parivar elsewhere in Gujarat. Tejgadh took five days to react and Panvad nearly nine days. Besides, awareness about Kashmir, Ayodhya, and cross-border terrorism has been almost negligible in the tribal villages. Many villages in the region have sarpanches who are illiterate or semi-literate; and the electronic media is almost absent in these villages.

During those days, one educated young Rathwa friend sent a note to me. It contained his reflections on the demise of a tree. This was the giant neem called Limda in Gujarati, and which gave the name 'Limdi Bazaar' to the area in which arson was going on. The neem was set on fire by the arsonists. It had been standing there for more than a century; and it was burnt alive. It burnt for ten days, slowly, ritually. The note sent to me by Arjun Rathwa said:

> Did the Limda have any religion apart from giving shade to the wayfarers? Was it not like an adivasi, neither Hindu nor Muslim? Why have they destroyed it? Was it anybody's enemy? Adivasis too are being destroyed like the neem. They are neither Hindus nor Muslims. But now they are being uprooted altogether.

I would like to consider this note as typical of the tribal non-involvement in communal politics. What, then, was the source of the wrath let loose on the Muslim community? The most viable answer to this question is that the tribals were made to fight a proxy war on behalf of the baniyas.

V

Two incidents from the earliest days of the Gujarat riots will illustrate the tribal unwillingness to participate in the communal frenzy. On the evening of 27 February, a truck carrying Muslim passengers from Panchmahals sped through Tejgadh, causing another vehicle, a jeep carrying passengers, to pull closer to the edge of the road. Such jeeps, the most popular mode of transport in the area, are impossibly over-crowded, and passengers hang on to the vehicle on all sides. This one swerved so close to the edge of the road that four passengers, three men and a woman, died on the spot, crushed between the vehicle and the trees on the side of the road. The villagers knew that the other vehicle, which had caused the accident, was carrying Muslims, not from any other district but from Panchmahals, not on any other day but the day of the Godhra outrage. Yet the villagers in Tejgadh allowed the vehicle safe passage with no expression of anger, which under the circumstances would have been justified even on an ordinary day.

The second incident took place on 28 February in Haridaspur, the oldest segment of Tejgadh. Haridaspur has 170 households, all linked through a clan relationship. The people of Haridaspur had gathered during the forenoon to cremate and mourn the death of an inhabitant. In that assembly of approximately 1,200 people, some of the elected members of the panchayat from another locality had been talking of avenging the Godhra incident. But their inflammatory appeals found no favour, even after the gathering had been served the ritual drink of wine. This was the support, or lack of it, to Hindutva appeal on the day on which all newspapers carried headlines about the Godhra carnage. Persons present at the cremation have reported to me (on conditions of anonymity) that an announcement was made that free supplies of kerosene and liquor would be made available to those who had the 'courage' to attack Muslims.

The sarpanch of Tejgadh was approached by the troublemakers on 1 March and his participation sought in burning Muslim families; he is reported to have refused to allow any violence within the limits of his panchayat. It appears that on 2 and 3 March, the communal section of the village changed its argument by giving up the purely communal angle and bringing in the more acceptable business angle. It said that the Muslim businessmen had become too arrogant and, to use the equivalent of the local idiom, that 'they have put on too much fat'. This argument clinched the issue; and on the evening of 4 March, when Chief Minister Modi contended that 'the riots had been brought under control within a record seventy-two hours', the first Muslim shop was set on fire.

This shop was owned by 55-year-old Yakub Khatri and had wares like biscuits and mints. Yakub Khatri owned 5 acres of agricultural land and his brother Ghanibhai was a respected figure in the affairs of the Tejgadh mosque. However, the sweetmeat shop does not give a clear picture of Yakub's financial status. He owned a large house and more shops, selling foodgrains, cutlery, bangles, and shoes, at a distance of 800 metres. Obviously, by targeting Yakub Khatri, it was possible for the Hindu communal force to combine the theme of religious revenge with that of business competition.

During this instance of arson, the Muslim community in Tejgadh was still present in the village. It tried to counter the attack, but the mob that had gathered was large, and its resistance could not have been adequate. There were no policemen present at the scene of this crime. Quite obviously, over the three preceding days, the Muslims in Tejgadh had feared such an attack and had already prepared themselves to flee. The riots that began during the late hours of the afternoon continued during the evening, with two more shops gutted by fire. During the night, all the Muslims fled. No one seemed to know where they had sought asylum. It was rumoured that during the Yakub Khatri episode, Muslims had fired shots at the mob, implying that they were in possession of unlawful weapons and strengthening the stereotype of all mosques being places for hoarding weapons.

The next shop destroyed was owned by Kadarbhai, aged fifty-five, and owner of a flour mill, a cloth shop, and a grocery shop. Dilawarbhai, aged forty, who owned a cloth shop and an adjacent shop selling cutlery and shoes, was next in the line of fire. Ahmedbhai, fifty-five, owned a foodgrains business and also hired out materials like pandals and public address systems for public functions. Nasirbhai, who also had a cutlery and foodgrains business, followed in line. At this juncture, the communal interest seems to have faded from the minds of the rioters. Those who organised and funded the riots appear to have started viewing this operation purely as a business activity of eliminating the competition and creating a total control over the market; and those who participated in the riots appear to have started viewing the incidents as an opportunity to loot in the manner of an unusual public ritual. I have already commented on the ritual aspect of the Tejgadh riots and how it was appropriated by the Panvad riots, which were just about breaking out at this juncture.

It was also at this juncture that the five rumours listed previously were planted, because an internal contradiction had started breaking up the momentum which the communal force had managed to create with great difficulty. The contradiction appears to have emerged from the intention of the tribals to attack businessmen (who invariably have been moneylenders), and the baniya intention of causing an attack on Muslim businessmen alone. The Hindu baniyas behind the riots started fearing that the tribal enthusiasm for looting shops would lead to their own shops becoming targets. Therefore, once again the riot machine at Tejgadh chose to burn down the two shops belonging to Yakub Khatri which had been spared during the first round of arson. It appears that owing to Yakub's familial tie with Gani, an attack on him looked like an attack on the Tejgadh mosque.

The next to be attacked was an elderly and respectable Muslim popularly known as Lakhpati (meaning millionaire), who had been a kingpin in the local moneylending business (although his fortunes had been sinking in recent years). When communal passions were ignited, the rioters had no time to think of the financial status of their victims. Therefore, the houses of Bhikha the tailor, Fakirbhai the poor peasant with a landholding of less than an acre, and that of Yusufbhai Khatri, a retired prison clerk, were reduced to ashes. But the business interest in the riots did not wane at all; and therefore a warehouse where Muslim merchants used to stock their wares was also set on fire. The houses that the Muslim inhabitants had deserted were searched by the mobs and vandalised. The last to be attacked was Basheer Khatri's shop, which sold soft drinks and cloth. The police presence in Tejgadh throughout the days of the riots, a long period of two weeks, was more marked by its complicity than by its inadequacy. The most explicit comment on the motive and nature of the riots comes from the fact that not even once after 4 March did the panchayat members or the local Hindu baniyas make an attempt to dissuade the rioters.

Their only act of 'grace' was to spare the house of Shabirbhai, who has been an elected member of the panchayat and represents, at present, the Muslim community in Tejgadh. Thus, the 500-odd Muslim inhabitants of Tejgadh were 'punished' for someone else's attack on the S6 coach of the Sabarmati Express at Godhra, and more importantly, for competing with the Hindu moneylenders in the tribal area. Similarly, throughout the few days of intense rioting in Panvad, one repeatedly heard that the riots were meant to teach the lesson of their lives to the Muslim moneylenders, who had 'put on too much fat'.

VI

It would be completely wrong to assume that rioting in these tribal villages was, at any stage, in support of Hindutva. The facts show that this is far from the truth. There had to be a considerable amount of coaxing before any tribal village joined in the riots. There was free use of intimidation, too. Generally, a group of fifteen to twenty persons went to the sarpanch of a village to ask him to supply forces for attacking Muslims. One or two of the ringleaders did the speaking: they promised protection from the law to all those who joined them and threatened those who refused the 'invitation'. Since the instigators belonged to the ruling party, it was very intimidating to encounter such promises and threats. Before and during the main days of the Panvad riots, a young Rathwa—who became the Shaman in the widespread rumour—promised Rs 2,00,000 to those families who suffered a casualty in the rioting. Alternatively, he would threaten those who refused with dire consequences. As it happened, this Rathwa had neither the wealth to ensure the promised compensation, nor the political clout to carry out the threats.

It must also be kept in mind that Rathwas are a people of very few words; they do not speak beyond a monosyllable in their normal conversation, and very rarely tell lies. Police often say that if a Rathwa commits a murder, he will report it to the police station himself and confess to his crime. Therefore, when this person was going around making the offer, he was, in all probability, not using empty words. Surely other persons with more money to offer had backed him, and he was clearly working at their behest. All in all, therefore, the tribal riots seemed to be organised by the moneylenders, even though legal evidence to establish this fact will be slow in coming. The combing operation taken up by the state following the riots was probably a superficial exercise, ending with a large number of poor rioters being booked under the law on the basis of stolen goods, such as utensils, foodgrains, and cloth, found in their dwellings.

There have been excellent studies on the role of the *sahukar* in the Panchmahals during the nineteenth century, and on how they generated the tribal resistance movement in order to protect their own right to trade in salt in the Sirohi district of Rajasthan.[1] Thanks to these studies, one can say with certainty that the tribals in western India have remained under the yoke of the moneylender for centuries.

Particularly from the time that the tribals lost their sovereign rights over the forests and had to identify themselves with a given piece of land which was recorded in the books of the Revenue Department, their ability to meet any contingencies requiring large cash payments has gone down considerably. The land available for cultivation gets divided with every passing generation, although such divisions are not necessarily reflected in the land records. In rain-fed agriculture, the tribal tiller manages to produce just enough for subsistence, and even a single year of poor rains leads to endless indebtedness. Bank operations in tribal areas have been shamefully anti-tribal. In the first place, the service branches are not easily accessible in terms of their geographical location. Even when they do exist, their operations have no place or thought for the tribals, despite directives from the zonal offices and agencies like the National Bank for Agriculture and Rural Development (NABARD). A tribal with whom a bank manager has entered into any conversation is indeed fortunate. There is rarely a tribal who is not insulted when he enters a bank. Then there is the documentation aspect of any bank deal, which is beyond a tribal to cope with.

As against this, the private moneylender asks for no documents. He knows every tribal who comes to him as a client by name. His terms are sufficiently flexible to accommodate modifications in the schedule of payment, should it be required due to a failure of the monsoon. In exchange for all this kindness, the moneylender charges a high rate of interest. It ranges from Rs 5–12 per month, that is, 60–144 per cent a year. The interest for the first three months is deducted from the principal at the time of the lending, which means that an amount of Rs 70 is handed over to the borrower out of a notional Rs 100 if the interest is 120 per cent. The loan is not required to be repaid in cash; the moneylender accepts foodgrains, forest produce or timber in lieu of cash, at a rate that he will decide according to the going rate in the local market. If the foodgrains are not enough to repay the loan with the interest, the borrower approaches another moneylender in order to procure the cash to repay the first loan in full. Two centuries of this lending practice have made the moneylenders prosperous beyond imagining, and the tribals indebted beyond redemption.

The moneylenders reside in the larger villages like Tejgadh or Panvad, or in towns where the weekly *haat* is held. The tribal peasants go to the *haat* every week and make it a point to wish the moneylenders. This, they think, adds to their creditworthiness. Their location helps them to keep an eye on the economic transactions of the borrowers, as most of them take place in the market or else are discussed by their fellow villagers.

The politicians too are greatly dependent on the moneylenders for their political success, for the *sahukar*s control the vote banks for them. It is almost impossible for politicians to not be sensitive to the views and interests of the moneylenders. Even when the elected representatives of people belong to the tribes in the areas with reserved constituencies, they are severely restricted from undertaking developmental activities that will harm the interests of the moneylenders. Therefore, while one finds that an impressive developmental activity of a cosmetic nature takes place in tribal areas, economic empowerment is deliberately given a back seat. Poor infrastructure, chronic cash-crunch, pervasive unemployment, illiteracy, and technological backwardness, which in other sectors are considered unfavourable for economic growth, are the necessary and minimum conditions for growth in the private moneylending sector. The situation may differ in degree from one tribal district to another, but the general pathology of tribal underdevelopment and chronic indebtedness does not.

VII

About a decade ago, when I began my study of tribal languages and culture, I was unaware of the power of the moneylender in tribal society. Former Governor of the Reserve Bank and Director of the London School of Economics, I. G. Patel, had remarked to me in 1996: 'Once you start making an economic intervention in tribal life, you will come up with massive opposition.' Therefore, when a Trustee of the Bhasha Research Centre, Ravikant Joshi, suggested that we introduce a micro-credit scheme for tribals in Tejgadh, I wanted to look for a non-radical cover for taking anything so radical to the tribals. We found that the Rotary Club in Baroda was ready to collaborate. But soon the Rotarians grew tired of operational difficulties; but we found, on the other hand, that the tribals enthusiastically joined the scheme. The next requirement was to create a channel for the sale of their agricultural produce without the agency of the middleman. So we brought in Trifed, a corporation established by the Union government specifically for this purpose. This was too much of a threat for the grain merchants and the moneylenders. I remember how angry they were with me and how they threatened a hunger strike if I did not instantly abandon the Trifed operation.

But even at that time, I was not aware of the real cause of the anger, which became clear as the micro-credit scheme progressed and expanded. Gradually, I started hearing that both the Congress and the BJP were against our activity, and politicians from both sides started making angry representations against our activities in the high offices in Gandhinagar. At least two successive District Magistrates of Vadodara asked me to focus only on language research and not do extension work involving activities like micro-credit. 'There is a strong opposition to your work and it will increase in future,' they said. Having experienced the intensity of the moneylenders' anger, I am not surprised that it has been the most focal cause of the brutal attack on the Muslim moneylenders. This could have been averted had the spirit of the Constitution been taken into consideration by those in whom the Constitution vests certain special powers for the welfare of the weaker sections.

By March 2000, I had become fully convinced that the problem of tribal indebtedness would result in a major upheaval if it was not tackled well in time. Therefore, I wrote to the Governor of Gujarat, Sundersinh Bhandari, drawing his attention to the problem and urging him to use his special powers under Article 5 (2,6) of the Fifth Schedule:

> During my work with tribal communities of Gujarat I have repeatedly come across the frightening phenomenon of long-term indebtedness. I have noticed that tribals have been borrowing sums from private moneylenders residing in taluka towns and commercial centres at an exorbitant rate of 80 per cent to 100 per cent interest in order to meet their needs of cash required at the beginning of the agricultural season or during weddings and festivals. They are invariably not able to pay back the interest let alone the original sum borrowed. Recently we formed 100 Self Help Groups under our Micro-Credit programme with a membership of about 1200 families. Our experience showed that without an exception, the families have been victims of the exploitative money lending system. On the basis of this survey and my earlier work in other tribal areas of Gujarat, I have come to the firm conclusion that no economic development of the tribals will be even remotely possible if nearly 4.5 million of the 7 million tribals in Gujarat are groaning under the burden of indebtedness.
>
> On behalf of these 4.5 million tribals of Gujarat somehow managing to survive and trying to be free from the acute indebtedness, I most sincerely appeal to you to use the powers vested in Governor's office under the provisions of the 5th Schedule, Part B, 5 (2,6) which states:
>
> 'The Governor may make regulations for the peace and good government of any area in a State which is for the time being a Scheduled Area.
>
> … such regulations may—

(c) regulate the earning on of business as moneylender by persons who lend money to members of the Scheduled Tribes in such area.'

I would further like to pray that all Scheduled Areas (inclusive of the 9 tribal sub-plan areas) be covered by the regulation.

The regulation should prevent from the date of the issuance of regulation lending of short term or long term loans, involving small or large sums, in cash or kind, by charging interest which is higher than the current bank rates of interest.

It should also declare all debts received by any tribal person null and void and not binding on the borrower in case such debts were received prior to the date of the issuance of the regulation.

The regulation should make lending of money or kind at the rate of interest which is higher than the prevailing bank rate of interest to tribal persons, a non-bailable criminal offence.

It is also necessary to place a general moratorium on all and every deed of land transfer for one full year from the date on which the regulation comes into effect.

I hope that Your Excellency will take a serious view of the exploitative practice and decide on the matter expeditiously. I have no doubt in my mind that in consonance with the spirit of the Constitution and in the interest of social justice, our State needs to bring a permanent end to a great social evil which has made tribal life a curse.

Subsequently, Mahasweta Devi, Bhupen Khakhar, and I met him to discuss the problem. He argued that there was not enough factual data to support our claim. Our argument was that moneylenders would not, on their own, submit their books of accounts to the government. The decision would have to be made on the basis of his discretion and understanding. He assured us that our petition would be sent to the Minister in Charge of Tribal Development. Then Mahasweta Devi sent a similar request to the President of India. No reply to our letters has ever been received.

VIII

The use of bows, arrows, and guns by the tribals against the police during the riots is not sufficiently explained by an analysis of their indebtedness to the moneylenders, and their being coaxed by the latter into eliminating the Muslim competitors. The mob-militancy of the Rathwa tribals has other sources. In order to explain these, we need to look at the sociology of Panvad more closely, and how its confrontation with modernity has produced unique discontents.

Among the tribal towns of Vadodara district, Panvad is closest to Madhya Pradesh. The Bhils, who are no different from the Rathwas in language or custom and who live on the other side of the completely notional border, were at one time notified during British rule under the Criminal Tribes Act (1871). The reason for this notification was that they had earlier worked as seasonal soldiers for the Maratha princes in Indore and Dhar. But their 'denotification' in 1952 has left them with no real choice either, a life of occasional crime being their only option. The possible menace of the denotified Bhils across the border have led the villages surrounding Panvad to launch into a massive deforestation of the low hills, in order to increase their range of visibility as a measure of security. The deforestation of this region was encouraged by the timber merchants at Chhota Udepur, who controlled the Forest Kamdar Sangh during the 1960s.

All the ecological dangers that follow deforestation have been visited upon the Panvad region. Agricultural income in that area is lower in comparison with the corresponding agricultural holdings in other tribal areas of the district. As a way out of this, Panvad tribals have moved hopefully towards literacy and education; but for want of an institution of higher learning in the near vicinity, the young tribals end up with a high school education and little or no employment. Many migrate to places like Surat to work as diamond cutters, and to Kutch to work as construction or agricultural labour. The Gujarat Mineral Development Corporation (GMDC) had, in nearby Kadipani, a mining project for extracting Calcium Fluoride, or fluorspar, to sell to ceramic and toothpaste industries. This had left the low hills of the tribal habitat devastated, with the waters of the tiny river there—forming a tributary to the Orsang river—yellow and unusable. However, for many years, this project used to provide employment. But some years ago, it ran into rough weather due to legal and administrative hassles. Since then, the young tribals in the area have taken to drug-trafficking and a small amount of arms-selling. The arms are brought in from Madhya Pradesh and taken to Vadodara, and the customers are then located in the region and directed to Vadodara for a bargain purchase. Those who make this easy money move on to becoming small-time moneylenders and start acquiring Hindu names and traits. They are the ones who become hospitable to various sect movements. These new arrivals in the Hindu fold have become the special constituency of the Hindutva movement in the area.

When we started the micro-credit scheme in 1999, we also formed Self-Help Groups (SHGs) of tribals in the villages surrounding Panvad. The groups were Kanalwa (2), Chimli (1), Dungargam (2), Shihada (17), Jhanjharjhol (7), Panvad (9), Modhalia (4), Rangpur (1), Jhakha (1), Kavra (14), Ganthiya (4), and Gabadiya (4). During the three years of drought, while the SHGs in other villages had great difficulty in repaying the small bank loans, these SHGs would suddenly come up with wads of bank notes and repay the loans of several groups on a single day. I was surprised to find, on many occasions, that the notes brought for repayment were serially numbered. Obviously they did not reflect collections from the poor tribals, which, in the case of the SHGs in other villages, used to come in the form of soiled and old currency notes such as labourers keep with them. Equally obviously, the money came from a bank withdrawal. The members of the SHGs had, in principle, no other bank accounts than the ones we were helping them to operate. It is only in retrospect that I can say that the amounts came from moneylenders, from a loan given to a group leader to bring the micro-credit scheme to a halt. The Panvad tribals were quite prepared to return to the 120 per cent interest rate from the bank's mere 12 per cent. For the young, neo-Hindu, semi-educated, unemployed, indiscriminate generation, the Hindu moneylender has become the role model, and drugs and unlicensed arms the new sources of a sense of power.

The ultimate source of violence is the mind and not the weapons in one's possession. The tribal mindset is not feudal, but it is certainly medieval. It is not feudal because of the tribal attitude towards State formation, in which the clan replaces the State. But in the interests of preserving clan autonomy and clan purity, the attitude towards women among the tribals is dictated by a limitless fear of the violation of women by outsiders. When, in rare cases, a tribal woman expresses her desire to marry a person outside the particular tribal clan, there is invariably bloodshed. While girls have the freedom to choose their life partners within the clan and without the slightest opposition from the family or relatives, they have no freedom to extend the choice beyond the male members of the clan. This social code, however, is coming increasingly under stress from the rapidly changing economic context.

The tribal district north of the Panvad–Chhota Udepur area, that is, the Panchmahals, has witnessed the social transition of women's status on an unprecedented scale. Among the tribals, dowry is given by the groom to the bride's parents. The bride-price among most tribes is nominal or notional. But among the heavily indebted Panchmahals tribals, this bride-price has come to be perceived as an alternate source of income. In recent years it has soared to Rs 60,000, while earlier it used to be Rs 1,000–2,000. The result is that as soon as the wedding takes place, the groom takes the bride with him to a city like Ahmedabad or Vadodara, and the two start working as labourers so that the huge amount borrowed from relatives and moneylenders can be repaid over a period of several years.

The condition of the migrant women labourers in the cities is pitiable. They have to face, among other things, sexual exploitation at the hands of the labour contractors and city dwellers. The tribals in Panchmahals have now started receiving lucrative offers from caste Hindus for the purchase of their daughters. The tribals in Panvad area are familiar with these changes. To the east of Panvad is Madhya Pradesh. The tribal women here have faced humiliation worse than those in the Panchmahals. Some of the denotified tribal communities such as the Bedias and Kanjars in that area have come to a situation where forcing young girls into sex work is seen as natural.

In the Panvad region, the fear of violation of tribal women has gripped the tribal psyche. The police records for the period 1990–2000 show that the highest number of murders in the region are related to the perceived fear of a woman being taken away. Therefore, it would have been surprising if the tribals in that region had not reacted violently after being fed a generous diet of rumours about fifty of their women being sexually abused by Muslims. This rumour was not used in Tejgadh by those who planned the pogrom, and therefore the scale of violence in Panvad was higher than in Tejgadh.

There is one more reason for tribal militancy in the area, but the scientific validity of this is not generally acceptable to sociologists. This reason originates in a biological condition resulting from a disease generally known as sickle cell anaemia. I became aware of the possible connection between the proclivity to violence and the genetic cell disorder when, as a Jawaharlal Nehru Fellow, I was working on a study of violence in India during the early 1990s (which forms the previous chapters of this book). At that time, the case of malnutrition of the Korku tribals in Amaravati district of Maharashtra had been receiving considerable media attention. About the same time, the Chandrapur tribal area in Maharashtra started showing a pronounced militant tendency. I followed the matter patiently for some years, and then decided to convene a conference of doctors, anthropologists, and researchers working on the sickle cell problem. Doctors from many countries, including Dr Kenneth Bridges of the Harvard School of Medicine, were present.

Since I am opposed to violence as a means of social change, and since I was aware of the alarming scale of the incidence of sickle cell anaemia in Chhota Udepur region, I approached District Magistrate Anil Mukim and presented the note to him in September 2000.

Anil Mukim thanked me for drawing his attention to the problem and told me that he had forwarded the note to the Health Secretary in Gandhinagar. On my part, I initiated several check-up camps with the help of Dr R. Z. Patel of Baroda Medical College for the detection of sickle cell patients, and started offering a relief supply of folic acid tablets to those detected with the condition.

IX

Those who want to understand the unexpected rise of violence among the tribals of Gujarat may find it useful to note that during a short period of six weeks preceding the March 2002 riots, in a small segment of Tejgadh, namely Haridaspur, with a population of 1,200, the following sudden deaths had occurred:

1. Mansukhbhai Dalasukhbhai, age 55
2. Chikhabhai Dalasukhbhai, age 45
3. Kanchanbhai Chhaganbhai, age 40

4. Kamriben Tersinghbhai, age 40
5. Maniabhai Ruplabhai, age 40
6. Singliben Nathiyabhai, age 55
7. Sansubhai Soriyabhai, age 13

In addition, two children aged ten and one died; their names are not on my record. Not all of them died of sickle cell. In fact, the general life span of sickle cell patients ranges between ten and twenty-five. Many of these therefore have to be described as deaths due to malnutrition and medical inattention. No government likes to accept the fact that many poor people die for want of a sufficient diet.

On 15 August 2001, there had been eight cases of starvation in Chhattisgarh, causing those tribals to eat a dead bullock's meat, which led to their deaths. At that time, I wrote to Prime Minister Atal Behari Vajpayee:

> On the Independence Day, as we were watching you speak to the nation, we also received the shocking news of the death of ten tribals in Chhattisgarh because of food poisoning caused after they ate the meat of dead bullocks. That tribals are driven to eating dead animals out of hunger which has no other means to assuage it is a shame for all of us who can get two square meals a day.
>
> This situation could have easily been averted, had the funds available for tribal development been put to use. Some days back I read a report in Gujarat *Samachar* that the Gujarat State has not used even one rupee from the grants available for tribal development during this financial year. A similar situation in Bengal is already being investigated by order of the Calcutta High Court after Smt. Mahasweta Devi filed a case. The Tribal Development Ministry of Central Government has mooted a foodgrains bank scheme; but I understand that its implementation in Orissa has been half-hearted and the scheme has more or less failed there. If your Government were to bring all the tribal villages under the foodgrains bank scheme in the States with tribal population, leaving out the Northeastern

> states, the total investments required would not exceed Rs. 800 crores (at Rs. 65,000 per bank as per the scheme). I, therefore, do not understand why your Government cannot provide food security to the tribals of India. The Korkus of Maharashtra have been dying of malnutrition; the tribal women in Rajasthan and Gujarat are being regularly sold for feeding their hungry families; the sickle cell anaemia which is already affecting nearly three per cent of tribal population, is further aggravated by want of adequate food. In Gujarat alone, where we have carried out testing, an estimated two lakh persons are awaiting slow but certain death due to the SCA. The situation of denotified tribals is even worse, because added to hunger they have to face persecution. If, under these circumstances, the Government remains passive, food security cannot be provided, what is the use of Independence for us?
>
> On my part, I have taken a vow to skip one meal a day throughout my life and to mobilise tribals in village to fight the oppressive situation till such a time as there is not even one hunger death among the tribals. I request you on behalf of the tribals of India to kindly do something concrete in this regard.

Subsequently, I met the prime minister on 13 September at his residence in Delhi, and emphasised the need to establish foodgrain banks in all tribal villages. Mahasweta Devi, Laxman Gaikwad, Haribhau Gaikwad, and Ajay Dandekar were present at the meeting, which lasted twenty-five minutes. I have learnt through newspapers that the Central government did declare the scheme of foodgrain banks for 1,16,000 villages. However, such foodgrain banks had not been established in Chhota Udepur prior to my pleading with the Union Tribal Secretary S. K. Naik and Commissioner for Tribal Development Ramji Rai. As a result of that campaign, forty villages of Chhota Udepur will get foodgrain banks from April 2002.

However, if a large section of the population is left to fend for itself and face poverty, hunger, and exploitation, and if their semi-literacy and unemployment lead them to a harsh zone of a conflict of social values, if the new role models are based on the idea of making easy money, it is more likely than not that a space for an irrational militant tendency will be created. Panvad could not have been an exception.

Yet, it would be wide off the mark to believe that the tribals in Chhota Udepur and Kawant talukas of Vadodara district had, at any time prior to the riots of March 2002, made any plans or conspiracy to launch an armed attack on the *haat*s in Tejgadh or Panvad, or that there was any leadership locally available with a political ideology which holds up violence as the means of social change.

On 13 March, District Magistrate Bhagyesh Jha and Senior DSP Keshav Kumar were shot at with a country rifle while they were in the field; and on 20 March, *The Times of India*[2] reported:

> ... After a week of skirmishes with the tribals, fifty-nine policemen were injured, two people killed, several houses charred, vehicles torched and shops looted ....
>
> Hordes of tribals would appear from the woods, make strange noises, rain arrows, pelt stones and vanish in thin air ....
>
> Even the convoy of District Collector Bhagyesh Jha and Senior Superintendent of Police Keshav Kumar was not spared.
>
> 'They appeared from nowhere and started shooting arrows. Later, gunshots were heard .... They made noises as if communicating among themselves and when we upped the defences they vanished ...,' Jha said.
>
> ... their strategy was evident in Kawant, Panvad and Bodeli .... the tribal used an innovative weapon .... referred to as an *'agni shastra'*—a 'fire bow', invented by attaching a rag soaked in fuel and setting it on fire seconds before shooting.

Another tactic attributed to the tribals is the use of poison-tipped bows. However, HQ Officer Parmar refuted the theory that a typical tribal aggressor dips his bow in a poisonous concoction before sending it through the spine of his victim. 'The bow heads are rusted and hence infect the wound. This is normally misconstrued as poison to make the bows more [deadly] …,' he said.

It is necessary to understand that guerrilla warfare is prompted by radical ideologies and is carried out over a long period of time in order to achieve ideological aims. The tribals in Panvad and Chhota Udepur have not developed any such ideology. To think of them as Naxalites will be a fatal mistake, because such a line of thought, echoed in newspapers several times, may actually create a stereotype that will lead to the creation of a movement where none exists. The violence in Panvad is clearly a case of rioting by a generation that has come under great economic stress and has decided to adopt the moneylender as the role model. Militant tribal movements are always *against* the moneylenders and landlords. In the case of the Panvad riots, the drive was basically to emulate the Hindu moneylender, and therefore the wrath was directed at the Muslim moneylenders and not the institution of *sahukari*. Such apparent or perceived militancy can easily be mitigated through appropriate economic measures leading to a general development of tribals. If, on the other hand, it is handled with no understanding or compassion, it will acquire an undesirable tone.

NOTES AND REFERENCES

1. See, for example, David Hardiman, 'The Bhils and Sahukars of Eastern Gujarat', in Ranajit Guha (ed.), *Subaltern Studies: Writings on South Asian History and Society*, Vol. V (New Delhi: Oxford University Press, 1987).

2. Sajid Shaikh, 'Tribals Fox Cops with Guerrilla Warfare Tactics', *The Times of India*, 20 March 2002.

3 The Birth of Dakshinayan

Indian Writers in Resistance

Dakshinayan

The term 'Dakshinayan' has several literal and symbolic meanings.

It is the moment when the sky is crowded with dark clouds. It is the time of the year when the nights are long and days short. It implies a southward journey.

In our time, it brings to mind the concerns that dominate the discourse in the global South. It certainly hints at turning away from easy paths of ascension and exploring new ways of relating to space and time.

Dakshinayan is a movement that has sprung up through a collective desire to forge a new solidarity between cinema, theatre, literature, and the arts.

It is a call for a fearless articulation of the desire to resist; a collective and spontaneous call to sensitive minds to defend the dignity of the human and the sanctity of the spiritual.

Dakshinayan is a new struggle for the freedom of creative expression that foregrounds tolerance and dialogue.

It is an attempt to deepen rational and progressive thinking as being pivotal to a society that is genuinely equal, just, and respectful of diversity.

Dakshinayan is the long awaited initiative to go beyond caste, class, creed, gender, language, form, and genre, to cross borders between identities, to nurture the imagination without narrow borders, and to celebrate the voice that frees the mind from limits imposed by ideologies, credos, partisan institutions, and movements.

It is a movement that asserts that the earth does not belong to us; rather, we belong to it.

Dakshinayan asserts that all that is, is significant.

Where the mind is without fear and the head is held high
Where knowledge is free
Where the world has not been broken up into fragments
By narrow domestic walls
Where words come out from the depth of truth
Where tireless striving stretches its arms towards perfection
Where the clear stream of reason has not lost its way
Into the dreary desert sand of dead habit
Where the mind is led forward by thee into ever-widening thought
and action
Into that heaven of freedom, my Father, let my country awake.

Rabindranath Tagore

THE MURDER OF M. M. KALBURGI

Assassinations are not new in India. Like elsewhere in the world, the elimination of persons whose thoughts are inconvenient to the dominant sections of society has, alas, been a phenomenon known to India. If ancient Greece had a Socrates and the ancient Jews a Jesus, eliminated by those who found their thought too disturbing, India had its Basava, Mira, and Tukaram in the same order of thinkers, who were similarly eliminated. In recent times, too, India has experienced the assassinations of the Father of the

Nation, Mahatma Gandhi, Prime Minister Indira Gandhi, and her son, Rajiv Gandhi, himself also a prime minister. These are the more prominent historical figures. Many others, relatively less known, have had to face their end by assassination. In the past few years, this method of dealing with one's thought adversaries has once again gained popularity, and India has seen a spate of what can be described as 'intellectual murders' or 'literary assassinations'. Narendra Dabholkar was killed in Pune in 2013, Govind Pansare in Kolhapur in early 2015, M. M. Kalburgi in Dharwad later that year, and Gauri Lankesh was 'knocked off' in Bangalore in 2018. The reason was simple: their thoughts were not convenient for those who killed them, and all four had felt that expressing themselves with a sense of freedom was a natural thing to do.

I had to visit Dharwad in the first week of August 2015. It is at best a sleepy academic town, devoted to music and literature. It is here that M. M. Kalburgi lived. Almost all of his 120-odd books were written during his years as Professor at Karnataka University in Dharwad, and the few years as Vice-Chancellor of Hampi University, a four-hour drive from Dharwad. My visit was occasioned by a memorial lecture for V. K. Gokak, a well-known Kannada writer-poet. When I was in Dharwad, Dr Kalburgi was still there. Three weeks later, I read in the newspapers that two young men had entered his house in the morning, shot him, and walked away. He was no more.

As literary critic Rajendra Chenni described,

> Prof. M.M. Kalburgi was an eminent scholar and researcher who contributed in a significant way to the development of modern research in the areas of Vachana writings, interpretation of inscriptions, study of folklore, archival work involving oral and documented resources of history (such as Kaifiyats), literary critical interpretation of major Kannada texts and ideological issues

> pertaining to Lingayat-Veerashaiva traditions, notions of Kannada and Karnataka. Even this list does not exhaust the heterogeneous fields of knowledge he explored. The numerous writings of Prof. Kalaburgi have been published in nine volumes of *Marga* ('The Path') running into about 4000 pages. Sadly, very few of his writings have been translated into English. Though his brutal assassination drew the attention of the entire world, not many are aware of the nature of his research and writings.[1]

On the day I read the news of his killing, memories of my Dharwad visit were still fresh in my mind. I felt perplexed; why would anyone think of murdering a scholar as meek as M. M. Kalburgi? I tried to call friends in Dharwad to find out what this was all about. The police had by then taken over the investigation; and the very first 'theory' they floated concerned a family feud involving property or land. Of course, the question of this scholar having any major property or amassed wealth just did not arise, so modest was his life.

The next day, I had to preside over a National Conference organised by the Sahitya Akademi—the Indian National Academy of Letters. This was in Nagpur, a good 1,100 km north of Dharwad. However, one expected that since Kalburgi was a one-time awardee of the Sahitya Akademi, there would be some expression of condolence, in keeping with the age-old practice in India. But there was none. In fact, any mention of the incident was quickly brushed aside in a hush-hush manner by most of those present, as if calling the murder a murder would offend some invisible eye watching us all. I was to preside over the inaugural part of the conference, and my turn to address the gathering came at the end of the session. I thought it would be proper to express my condolence to the literary community, which I did. I could notice, though, that not everyone present considered my action prudent, even though most in the audience rose to join me in observing a minute's silence.

As I travelled back from Nagpur to Baroda, my home town, my mind was trying to make sense of the unease amongst writers, something India had not known since the eighteen months of national Emergency during 1975–77. Yet I kept hoping that the Sahitya Akademi, being a body of writers, would be bold enough to issue a statement condemning the attack on Kalburgi. A week passed and nothing happened. Time went by, and by early October, I began feeling so suffocated that I considered it necessary to telephone someone in Delhi to ask the reason behind this deafening silence in the face of the brutal killing of one of the most distinguished literary scholars in the country. I kept waiting, with hope for clemency. Finally, when I realised that my hopes were to no avail, I felt it my moral duty to return the Akademi award I had received in 1993, a similar award with which the Akademi had honoured Dr Kalburgi. I thought this would be the most appropriate way of placing my protest in the Akademi's court. On 11 October, I sat down to write to the President and Vice-President of the Akademi. The following is the text that emerged from my tormented heart:

> It is with utmost regrets that I would like to convey to you that I wish to return the 1993 Sahitya Akademi Award given in the category of books in English to my work *After Amnesia* (1992). I do this as an expression of my solidarity with several eminent writers who have recently returned their awards to highlight their concern and anxiety over the shrinking space for free expression and growing intolerance towards difference of opinion. These eminent writers have already stated their concerns in statements sent to you as well as through media interviews and discussions. I need not, therefore, state again what has already been conveyed to you. However, I would like to add that I visited Dharwad in the first week of August, just three weeks before the shocking attack on the late Dr. M. M. Kalburgi which resulted in his death. I was there for delivering the First V. K. Gokak Memorial Lecture. You

may recall that the high office that you hold at present on behalf of the literary community of our country was at one time held, among many other mighty predecessors you are blessed with, by V. K. Gokak. He was the Principal of Willingdon College during the years of the Independence movement. On one occasion, when the police came to arrest students, he stood at the entrance of the college, blocked their entry and asked them to first arrest him before they touched the students. It was this kind of concern for freedom that he brought to the institutions he headed. I hope you do not think that he was not sufficiently pragmatic. When I gave the Gokak lecture, Dr. Kalburgi was still alive. Alas, he had to fall to the forces of intolerance. A week after his killing, I participated in a Seminar organized by the Sahitya Akademi. This was in Nagpur. I was to preside over the Inaugural Session. I was quite dismayed to see that the seminar began without a word of reference to the recent attack on a scholar honoured by the Akademi. Therefore, when my turn to speak came at the end of the session, I asked the audience if they would object to my observing a two minute silence to mourn the dastardly killing. Please note that all of them stood up in silence with me. If our writers and literary scholars had the courage to stand up in Nagpur, I fail to understand why at the Ravindra Bhavan there should be such a deafening silence about all that is happening to free expression in our country. I have personally known both of you as my seniors and have admired your writings and imaginative powers. May I make bold to say that your moment of reckoning has come? I hope you will give this country the assurance that it is the writers and thinkers who have come forward to rescue sense, good-will, values, tolerance and mutual respect in all past ages. Had this not been so, why would we be remembering the great saint poets who made our modern Indian languages what they are today? The great idea of India is based on a profound tolerance for diversity and difference. They far surpass everything else in importance. That we have come to a stage when the honourable Rastrapatiji had to remind the nation that these must be seen as non-negotiable foundations of India should be enough of a reason for the Sahitya Akademi to act.

THE WRITERS' DISCONTENT

I was aware that four or five other Akademi Award winners had taken a similar decision to return their awards. Till then, I had not spoken to any of them, nor did I know all of them (although I had heard of them, and read some of their works). I sent my letter to the Akademi by about 3 PM. In a couple of hours, most of the TV channels and newspapers had picked up the news. On the same day, another writer, Anil Joshi, returned his award. Coincidentally, Anil Joshi was not only from Gujarat, the state to which I belonged, but (as I learnt later) resided in the same city as myself, only a couple of kilometres from my home. I had not heard of him till then as he had returned from his stay in the UK only recently. The TV channels initiated discussions on the 'award returning phenomenon', which soon acquired a Hindi name, '*award-wapasi*' (*wapas* means back, or 'to give back'). Many of the commentators interpreted the act as an 'attempt to spread disaffection towards the State'. This is precisely the wording used in the Indian law related to 'sedition'. I was a little surprised at this interpretation, for I had understood my act as a protest against a literary body, and not against the country that I have loved so deeply for over six decades.

In the days that followed, the electronic media opened quite a tirade against the writers returning awards. The award *wapasi* debate continued for close to two weeks. During that brief time, many more Indian writers returned awards they had received from the Central Academy and State bodies. A few even returned the civilian honour of the Padmashree. Many filmmakers returned their national and regional awards, received for excellence. The upsurge in protest was not only unprecedented, but it was also unique. What was even more unique and unprecedented was the easy offence that the Government of India seemed to have taken. Ideally, governments do not intervene in the disputes and disagreements surrounding literary and art bodies in India. But the award *wapasi* was taken by the ruling party as a challenge to the prime minister. Spokespersons of the ruling party continued to censure and ridicule the artists and writers involved.

Significantly, some major scientists also issued statements in support of the freedom of thought and the scientific temper. An eminent scientist, Pushpa Bhargav, founder of the Centre for Molecular Biology, was lampooned during a TV debate. His opponent, a spokesperson of the ruling party, did not hesitate to ask Dr Bhargav if he had any credentials as a scientist at all. This was the fate of anyone who raised their voice to protest the atmosphere of fear that prevailed amongst writers, thinkers, and scientists. It is difficult to describe exactly the intimidating tactics; but I can describe the spread of the protest.

THE PARLIAMENT RESPONSE

Much after the 'award *wapasi*' had been replaced by other protests, a question was asked in the Lok Sabha—the Lower House of the Indian Parliament—by MP Om Birla of the Bharatiya Janata Party (BJP) on 6 February 2017. He asked if the government was aware that many renowned writers had returned the awards given to them for their exemplary work in the field of literature; and if so, what were the reasons for this action and who were these writers who had returned their Sahitya Akademi awards since 2015?

He also sought information on how many writers had 'accepted the Government's request to take back the awards'.

The official reply of the Minister of Culture Mahesh Sharma, addressed to the Speaker of the House, Sumitra Mahajan, was:

> Yes, Madam. The list of writers who have returned their Sahitya Akademi awards during the last three years is enclosed at Annexure. The writers claimed that there was an attack on their freedom of expression and the Akademi kept silent on the issue.
>
> Yes, Madam. The Akademi had convened a special Executive Board meeting on 23.10.2015 and 17.12.2015 in which Resolution had been passed requesting the writers to reconsider their decision.
>
> Sri Nand Bhardwaj, noted Rajasthani writer, has taken back his decision of returning the award.[2]

The reply also contained a list of the writers who had returned their awards. It read:

> HINDI
>
> 1 Uday Prakash, 2 Ashok Vajpeyi, 3 Krishna Sobti, 4 Mangalesh Dabral, 5 Kashinath Singh, 6 Rajesh Joshi,
>
> ENGLISH
>
> 7 G.N. Devy, 8 Nayantara Sahgal, 9 Keki Daruwalla
>
> GUJARATI
>
> 10 Anil Joshi
>
> PUNJABI
>
> 11 Waryam Singh Sandhu, 12 Surjit Patar, 13 Jaswinder, 14 Gurbachan Bhullar, 15 Atamjit Singh, 16 Baldev Singh, 17 Darshan Butter, 18 Ajmer Singh Aulakh, 19 Mohan Bhandari
>
> RAJASTHANI
>
> 20 Nand Bhardwaj, 21 Ambikadutt
>
> KANNADA
>
> 22 Kum Veerbhadrappa, 23 Rahamat Tarikere, 24 Devanuru Mahadeva
>
> KASHMIRI
>
> 25 Ghulam Nabi Khayal, 26 Margoob Banihali

URDU

27 Munawwar Rana, 28 Khaleel Mamoon

MALAYAM

29 Sara Joseph

ASSAMESE

30 Homen Borgohain, 31 Nirupama Borgohain

TELUGU

32 Katyayani Vidmahe

The Translation Prize

HINDI

33 Chaman Lal

KANNADA

34 G.N. Ranganatha Rao

MARATHI

35 Ibrahim Afgan

Yuva Puraskar

ENGLISH

36 Aman Sethi

PUNJABI

37 Pragat Singh Satauj

Bal Sahitya Puraskar

TELUGU

38 M. Bhoopal Reddy

Golden Jubilee Award

39 Mandakranta Sen[3]

Thirty-nine coveted awards had been returned to the prestigious literary body in the wake of the murder of M. M. Kalburgi. The scale of this protest was simply unprecedented. What is even more important is that the protest had not been organised by any individual or political party; it was an absolute literary response to the political climate in the country.

The poet Keki N. Daruwalla stressed in his letter to the President of the Sahitya Akademi that he was not prompted by any political ideology:

> I wish to make it clear that I have no party leanings. I was no lover of the corrupt UPA 2. People like the late Dabholkar were murdered during the previous dispensation .... the landscape that confronts the writer today is bleak .... Faces will continue to be blackened with paint and painters like M.F. Husain will be forced into exile. A writer like Taslima Nasreen will have to leave Kolkata under a leftist regime. Statesmen will continue to be praised for their nationalism 'despite' the fact they are Muslims. Mob murders will continue to be described as accidents.

WHAT THE WRITERS' DISCONTENT MEANS

Commenting on this in the last week of October 2015, I wrote in *The Times of India:*

> The sudden outburst of anguish from so many writers and artists over the last two weeks has taken the country by complete surprise ... Various political parties have commented on it by placing themselves as allies or adversaries ....
>
> The ... Indian Writers Discontent ... is not an organized movement, nor a conspiracy .... It is neither engineered nor is it planned by any political party, outfit, a social organization or a funding agency ....
>
> It is an expression of the need to re-imagine India, to humanize it, to sensitize it to the core of not just democracy but civilization itself. At the heart of our great democracy is the idea of diversity and respect for that diversity ....

> Democracy can be deepened by tolerance .... Civilization can be enriched by respect for life and other ways of looking at life. Writers today have stood up to remind the country that weakening the foundations of democracy will be at our own peril ....

My attempt was to point out that it may be a long time before we realise the full significance of this discontent, which is very much like the medieval literary movement led by the saint-poets.

THE ATTACK ON A FOLK SINGER

Soon after this, we received the chilling news of a 'sedition' case being slapped on a folk singer in the state of Tamil Nadu (a state ruled by Jayalalithaa of the All India Anna Dravida Munnetra Kazhagam [AIADMK]). This was not the first case of sedition in Tamil Nadu; we learnt that several hundred persons had had to face this earlier. Aghast, some of my literary friends and I issued a statement:

> We feel shocked to read media reports that the folk singer Kovan has been charged with sedition in Tamil Nadu for composing and circulating songs. Folk literature has been a clear mirror of popular sentiment and for several thousand years has worked as a vehicle of expression. Some of us have spent dedicated time in documenting and conserving folk literature of India; therefore, we feel particularly sad that rather than showing compassion and empathy to the voice of the people, the government of Tamil Nadu has used its might to silence the singer.
>
> We feel equally shocked and sad that in our neighbouring country, Bangladesh, two publishers of a rationalist thinker have been assaulted, one of them hacked to death and another shot at. This Taliban like treatment meted to publishers and writers

is to be condemned by all those who uphold scientific temper, rational thought, freedom of speech and tolerance necessary for democracy.

Today, the 1st November, is the birth anniversary of Narendra Dabholkar, a rationalist thinker from Maharashtra, who lost his life for being a rational thinker. We appeal to all those who respect free speech and rational thinking to condemn these attacks and work towards increased tolerance.

The signatories to this statement included Gujarati writers Uttam Parmar (Kim), Kanji Patel (Lunawada), Paresh Nayak (Ahmedabad), and Bharat Mehta (Baroda). Later, a few others also signed it. While we were discussing the statement, it occurred to me that my writer friends from Gujarat had not fully grasped the brutality involved in the killings of Dabholkar, Pansare, and Kalburgi. For them, while perturbing, these were still at the level of news. Therefore, I suggested that they and I should pay a visit to the bereaved families in Pune, Kolhapur, and Dharwad, respectively. They agreed readily. Some more friends from Mumbai expressed their desire to join this sojourn. Since we were to start from Ahmedabad and move southwards to Mumbai, Pune, Kolhapur, and Dharwad, I thought the journey could be best described as 'going south'. I picked up the term that would be understood with equal efficiency in Gujarati, Marathi, and Kannada, with no further need for explanation. That term was 'dakshinayan'.

A Journey South for Understanding

Our journey began on 23 November 2015. Filmmakers Manishi Jani and Paresh Nayak, poets Kanji Patel and Anil Joshi, and

Gandhian activist and educationist Uttam Parmar formed the group. A few others joined us in Mumbai and in Pune, yet more came together. Dr Dabholkar's network in Maharashtra is known as the Andha-shraddha Nirmulan Samiti (ANIS, or Committee for Eradication of Superstitions). The social purpose journal that he capably edited is called *Sadhana*, established long years ago by Sane Guruji, a great culture hero of Maharashtra. ANIS and *Sadhana* jointly organised a large meeting at the S. M. Joshi Socialist Foundation in Pune. The hall was full; I recall that there were about 400 persons in the audience. The major literary figures among the participants were Atul Pethe, Anil Joshi, Anosh Malekar, Arun Bhagwat, Dileep Jhaveri, Ganesh Visputay, Hamid Dabholkar, Ibrahim Afgan, Jayant Joshi, Kanji Patel, Manishi Jani, Mukund Taksale, Paresh Naik, Prabodh Parikh, Pradnya Daya Pawar, Pramod Munghate, Rajan Khan, Ramesh Oza, Sachin Ketkar, Sandesh Bhandare, Sandhya Taksale, Sanjeev Khandekar, Surekha Devi, Sushil Kandalkgaonkar, and Uttam Parmar. Anil Joshi read some of his poems. Manishi Jani, Uttam Parmar, and Kanji Patel made some spirited speeches. I spoke at length about the facade of development in Gujarat and the spread of fear in the minds of the people. The applause was thunderous.

From Pune, we travelled to Kolhapur that evening and met the Pansare family—Govind Pansare's widow Umatai, who had been wounded during the attack, and his daughter-in-law Megha, a professor of Russian at Shivaji University. My writer friends spoke to them with moist eyes. We then met the others who had been working with Comrade Pansare for years. In the evening, we addressed a small gathering at the city centre. We were to set out for Dharwad, 200 km south of Kolhapur, the next morning. During the night and early in the morning, more writers and poets from different districts of Maharashtra came to join us. In Dharwad, on the evening of 26 November, a large number of writers from Goa joined us. By now, we were nearly 45 persons. We met Dr Kalburgi's widow on the morning of 27 November and later addressed a large gathering of writers from Karnataka—nearly sixteen of them had returned one or the other award—at the spacious auditorium of the Vidya Vardhak Sangh. Speeches were made in languages like Kannada, Marathi, Gujarati, Konkani, Hindi, and English.

By now, we had acquired the character of a multilingual, multi-state group of writers against fascism. We did not feel the need to introduce one to the other in that group. We all knew that we belonged together, belonged to the idea of an inclusive India that is tolerant, multicultural, multilingual, and patient with difference. Kannada tribal activist and CPM State Secretary G. N. Nagraj later sent a report he had prepared of this meeting. I present it in his words:

> On November 27, a unique meet was held in Dharwad, the place where Prof. Kalburgi was recently murdered. Writers who had returned their awards to Sahitya Akademi and various other academics and government servants from four states came together to tell the people why they had returned their awards. The occasion was the birthday of Prof. Kalburgi. A group of writers from Gujarat under the leadership of Dr Ganesh Devy who had returned his Sahitya Akademi award, started a yatra from their state which they called Dakshinayan. They were joined by a group of cinema producers, actors, painters from Mumbai. They visited the houses of Dabholkar and Pansare on his birthday and conducted meetings in both Pune and Kolhapur which were widely attended by literary persons, artists and scientists. In all these meetings, they explained why they had returned their awards.
>
> Then they proceeded towards Dharwad to meet the family of Prof. Kalburgi. In Dharwad, another stream from Goa joined them along with the writers of Karnataka. And it became a river as they travelled through the streets of Dharwad. They visited

Prof. Kalburgi's house and offered their condolences to his wife, son and daughter.

In the dialogue with the press and in the seminar organised by Prof. Kalburgi Hatya Virodhi Samithi of Karnataka, they declared in unequivocal terms that they will carry on the fight against intolerance and attack on freedom of expression and spread it to all corners of the country. In the second leg of their journey, they will continue their Dakshinayan to reach the southernmost point i.e., Kanyakumari. They would travel to Kerala, Tamil Nadu, Andhra Pradesh and Telangana.

Dr Ganesh Devy explained what caused him to decide to return the award. He said he was presiding over a seminar in Nagpur organised by Sahitya Akademi itself when the news of heinous murder of Kalburgi reached him. But the authorities of the Sahitya Akademi did nothing, not even offered a minute of silence as a form of condolence. Then he had to announce that he would be offering his condolence on his own and stood silently for a minute. Then the entire audience stood up and offered condolences. It was then that he decided to return his awards. From then on, he was pestered by many including journalists to question his decision and was charged that he was maligning the country's name. He asked which act maligned the country. Whether it was murder of Dabholkar, Pansare and Kalburgi which maligned the country or return of awards?

Another Sahitya Akademi award winner, Anil Joshi from Gujarat who is a famous Gujarati poet declared that they have taken up a Swachh Bharat Abhiyan but this is a Swachh Bharat Abhiyan of the minds of people. Then the artists film makers and directors from Mumbai, writers from Goa who had worked with Kalburgi on a project of translation of Vachanas of Lingayat saints into Konkani, writers who had returned their awards like Sri Rahamath Tarikere, Prof. RK Hudugi, director of Rangayana and president of Samudaya and Sri Iliger, also from Samudaya, both of whom returned their Sangeet Natak Akademi awards, K Neela who had returned her Kannada Sahitya Parishad award, Muddu Theertha

Halli, a seventeen years old, youngest of the writers to return award from Karnataka, all of them received a standing ovation from respected writers and audience. They explained how they were pained by the limitations imposed on the freedom of expression and how they were maligned by communal forces.

Finally it was declared by Dr Ganesh Devy that on January 30, the martyrs day on which Gandhiji was shot, a national meet of all the writers and artists who have returned their awards and who have raised their voice of protest against the attack on freedom of expression will be organised in Dandi from where Gandhiji started his famous Dandi march for salt satyagraha. This announcement was met with an uproar of welcome from the audience. Literary personalities from Karnataka declared there itself that they will start a Dandi yatra in thousands, in remembrance of the satyagrahis from Karnataka who had joined the Dandi march of 1930.

It was at this meeting that I voiced the sentiment that had been articulated by most of those who joined the Dakshinayan sojourn—that writers from all four states (Karnataka, Goa, Maharashtra, and Gujarat) should meet soon at some symbolic place. I thought of Dandi; and rather spontaneously, I declared that we would hold a Dakshinayan meeting—a *sarv-bhasha-samvad*—at Dandi on 30 January 2016. The response to that announcement was tremendous, to say the least. K. Neela from Gulbarga took the stage and shouted the slogan, '*Chalo* Dandi' (Let us march to Dandi). Everybody echoed her words, repeatedly. Yet, saying it and making it happen were two different things. I had to explain in the call for Dandi that Dakshinayan was not organised by any political party or organisation directly or indirectly affiliated to any political party. It was not funded by any Indian or foreign funding agency. It was an entirely voluntary and self-supported initiative by the individuals involved in it. But before I move forward, I shall say something more about Dandi.

DANDI AND DHARWAD

Soon after Gandhi moved to Ahmedabad after returning from South Africa, an extraordinary person entered his life and remained an important part of it till his very last breath. This was Mahadev Desai, a young man born in 1882 at Sarav in south Gujarat and a graduate from Bombay University. Mahadev Desai met Gandhi for the first time in 1915 and moved into the Ashram in 1917, when he was thirty-five. He maintained a diary of Ashram life, of all major events in Gandhi's life, his conversations and visitors, his trials and triumphs from November 1917 till a day prior to his sudden death from a heart attack on 15 August 1942. There was nothing that Gandhi did or thought that Mahadev did not know about, so tuned was his mind and being with the Mahatma's life.

Mahadev Desai was married before he moved into the Ashram. His son Narayan was born in December 1924. Narayan did not pursue any formal schooling, but grew up at the Sabarmati Ashram and then at Wardha, imbibing the great open university that the Mahatma himself was.

As a child, he played in the lap of Gandhi and became part of the collective, and as a young lad, he helped Gandhi in his satyagrahas. Drawing inspiration from Gandhi, Narayan and his wife moved to Vedchhi in south Gujarat to provide education to rural children. Although he was himself involved in the Bhoodan movement, worked closely with Vinoba Bhave, and subsequently led various peace movements, Narayan Desai remained committed to Vedchhi. It is there that he established the Sampurna Kranti Vidyalaya and wrote his remarkable books, including a major four-volume biography of Gandhi (now available in English translation) and a touching biographical narrative of his remarkable father Mahadev, *Agnikundama Ugela Gulab* (available in English translation under the title, *The Fire and The Rose*).

Gandhi, his chronicler Mahadev, and the writer-activist Narayanbhai Desai formed a great saga of protest spread over a century, a protest that sought life impulses and the force of love through the pursuit of truth. Dandi was its great symbol and fearlessness was at the heart of that saga of protest.

I had heard of Narayanbhai earlier, but it was in March 1994 that I met him for the first time. This was at the Kamani Auditorium in Delhi, where I had gone to receive the Sahitya Akademi Award for my English book. He was there to receive the award for his Gujarati work on the life of Mahadevbhai. The writers receiving the awards were seated according to the names of the languages, arranged in the Roman alphabetical order. As, in that order, 'E' (for English) came immediately before 'G' (for Gujarati), there being no scheduled language beginning with 'F', I found myself seated next to him. I was about a quarter century younger, and quite shy. He made the effort to start a conversation. We were together, as I remember, the next morning, when we had to speak on our respective books. He spoke in a very likeable Hindi. I was expected to speak in English, as an author awarded for an English book. Our mutual conversation was in Gujarati. His affable smile left a deep imprint on my memory. His simplicity clearly stated that he was a man wedded to Gandhian idealism. I knew of Mahadevbhai as the Mahatma's dedicated associate for long years, as his translator, as a person of rare historical significance. But I was unaware that he had a son and that I would get the opportunity to meet him in person. The moment within which we met was precious; given that, it was impossible for my mind to allow those memories to fade.

Several years passed, but I had no opportunity to meet him again. Two years after the meeting in Delhi, I decided to move out of Baroda University and make Tejgadh my destination. The literary references within which I had lived till then changed altogether. In March 1998, the Bangla writer Mahasweta Devi and I started working together, travelling long distances to meet nomadic communities. Her visits to Baroda increased in frequency. It was in 1999 that I received a postcard from Narayanbhai, asking me to meet him on one of his visits to Baroda. I did so. Our discussion was focused on Mahasweta Devi, for whom he had the utmost respect. On her next visit to Baroda, I drove her to Vedchhi so she could meet Naraynbhai. They were both happy beyond words, as only two kindred souls in mutual admiration can be.

Five years later, I invited Narayanbhai to visit Tejgadh, where the construction of the first building of the Adivasi Academy had been completed. That was on 15 August 2005. It was also the anniversary of Mahadevbhai's death in jail at the Aga Khan Palace, sixty-three years ago.

The rains were heavy that year and a small stream outside the Adivasi Academy campus had swollen into a ferocious rapid. Narayanbhai, though, waded through with ease. A year and a half earlier, his monumental biography of Gandhi had been published. It marked an unprecedented high point in the history of Gujarati literature and publishing, with several copies sold in record time. He had, by then, conceptualised the Gandhi Katha. We spoke of ways to have the biography translated into English.

Probably a year before this, I had decided to create a platform for the adivasi voice by asking them to assemble at Dandi on 1 May every year. It was decided that everyone would go there on bicycles. We requested Narayanbhai to bless the 'yatra' at Vedchhi, and he agreed to do so. After being blessed by him, we left for Dandi. This practice was continued in the years that followed. After a couple of years, Narayanbhai expressed his desire to join us at Dandi, and did so. That year, our theme was Adivasi Sahitya. Writers from numerous adivasi communities from all parts of the country had gathered there. He made an inspiring speech on the occasion.

Narayanbhai told me about the Gandhi Katha just as I had read about it in the media and heard reports through friends. However, I had not found the time to go and listen to him. It was in Baroda that I heard one of his 'katha' performances, and the truth hit me immediately—Narayanbhai had invited upon himself the unique blessing and burden of having to represent Gandhi in person. I say this because Narayanbhai himself was a great writer. Had he not been brought up the way he was, and had he not been Mahadevbhai's son, he would still have left a mark on public memory, given his acute power of observation, analysis, and recall, combined with his magic with words. Therefore, even though he thought of the self-effacement involved in representing Gandhi as his '*seva*' or '*bhakti*'—his sole *paramartha*—the sacrifice of his 'self' was enormous and is reason enough for history to remember him.

In 2010, I organised a large language conference in Baroda. Narayanbhai was obviously my choice for chief speaker. As was his habit, he asked me to allow all other speakers to speak first. He said he would first listen, and then respond. That morning, a dozen passionate speeches were made, urging the gathering to preserve linguistic diversity. Everybody then marched to Sayaji Garden in Baroda in a 'language diversity procession'. Narayanbhai walked ahead of everyone with a placard in hand. At the Sayaji Garden, as the sun went down and the evening shadows grew thicker, he and Mahasweta Devi lit 800 little lamps, one each for those 800 Indian languages that have come under assault from forces emerging from all quarters. Then Narayanbhai spoke, every word filled with clarity, compassion, and care. He touched the hearts of everyone present as a mother's love would touch an infant, beyond words. My path has indeed been shaped by his words.

In 2006, I was drawn into a controversy because of my rather candid comment on the economic and cultural attitudes of Gujaratis. This brought a deluge of censure from the literary community of Gujarat, which had by then learnt the necessity of being 'correct'. That year, the Gujarati Sahitya Parishad was to hold its annual conference at Tejgadh. Since my name was associated with the Adivasi Academy of Tejgadh, the proposed venue of the conference, the organisers decided to back out of the commitment. This too came under media discussion. Perhaps two years later, Narayanbhai was elected to preside over the Sahitya Parishad. Soon after, he made a personal visit to the Adivasi Academy to symbolise an end to the boycott. He made it a point to invite Mahasweta Devi to address the Parishad's annual meeting, and asked me to introduce her to the Gujarati literary community. For those who cared to understand, his message was clear.

I have had some very intense and rather personal conversations with Narayanbhai during the past two decades. He has often expressed his own dismay and disappointment, although they never related to his personal life or comfort. Instead, these related to his worry at the lack of inter-language dialogue, the neglect of India's villages, and about Gandhian institutions.

Narayanbhai's political sense was enviably sophisticated. He did not have to be involved in a movement in order to grasp its significance, tenor, strengths, and flaws. He instinctively knew their meaning and could articulate it with an amazing economy of words.

A few months before he died, Narayanbhai had composed a letter. Although he wrote elegant Gujarati as well as English, he chose to compose it in Hindi (or rather, Hindustani) as it was not intended for just academic Gandhians, writers, and intellectuals. He had in his mind a much wider audience for his letter, spread across villages in several states. Normally, his letters were written on postcards; but this time, it was placed in the brown envelope that the Sampurna Kranti Vidyalaya uses for its dispatches. He knew that it would be somewhat risky to send the contents on an open postcard. He sent this letter to all of his friends and colleagues who had worked with him in various movements. I too received it. When I read its contents, it saddened me to think that the son of Mahadev Desai, the Mahatma's closest associate, had to write this letter at the age of ninety, when he should have been thinking of putting together his memoirs. Here is a translation:

Narayan Desai,
Sampoorna Kranti Vidyalaya,
Gandhi Vidyapith, Vedachhi,
District Tapi, 394641

'*Priay Mitra, Saprem Jay Jagat*!
Dear Friend,
Affectionate 'May Life Triumph',

I decided to write this letter in the wake of the Lok Sabha election results. I have been advised to wait and to see how things develop before I write. I think, this letter too offers a moment for reflection. Therefore, it may be appropriate to express oneself without waiting too long.

The most serious concern is about the leader of the party that has won. So far his style of functioning has shown a close similarity with the fascist style. 1. It has aligned itself with a certain affluent class. 2. His oratory has helped in creating a favourable atmosphere. 3. Complete support has been obtained from the institution that is probably the most extensive and governed. 4. Most of the media has been bought over. 5. The forces with which one could fight the tendency have become largely hollow within.

Previously, the direction in which the future of the nation was depicted was cultural nationalism or religion. Later, the term 'development' was brought in; there is little difference between this idea of development and the idea of development offered by the Congress. Both are influenced by those powers that can soon bring the world close to extinction. The rapidly growing middle class in

> our country seeks to see a utopia in this 'development'. Fascism has won with its support, and this class will in no time become submissive and a cowardly intellectual class. The international atmosphere and the global economic regime can pretty soon push the world to the brink of war.
>
> The question is what should be the first duty of the 'Power of Life?'
>
> We have to think if any new forms of energy are sprouting up in the country, such forms that can help change the direction, such that do not spend themselves in despising each other, such impulses that may not give an altogether new direction but at least prevent the nation from a down fall ....

The letter continues and, after offering his comments on the potential of various social classes—the youth, dalits, tribals, and women—and the ideas of Mahatma Gandhi, J. C. Kumarappa, Vinoba Bhave, Schumacher, and Jai Prakash Narayan, and after reminding the reader that he would soon complete the ninetieth year of his life, Narayanbhai expressed his hope that 'these thoughts may initiate some new impulses'. I do not know if he received very many responses from those to whom he sent this letter. A few months after he wrote the letter, he went into a coma; and although he came out of it for a brief period, he passed away soon after.

Narayan Desai passed away in March 2015. Throughout the months of September and October, filmmakers, artists, scientists, and writers from all parts of India came out in a variety of ways to express their sentiments in response to the atmosphere prevailing in the country. The protest came under attack and these writers and artists were depicted as lacking in national pride, patriotism, and love for the leader. They were heckled during television debates and mocked at and ridiculed in the media.

I had written in the announcement of the Dandi meet:

> The Sarva-Bhasha-Samvad convened at Dandi on 30 January 2016 is an entirely voluntary expression of creative and sensitive minds. It is not sponsored or funded by any organisation. It is not initiated, promoted or supported by any political party or party affiliate, nor is it directed against any particular political party. It is an attempt to reflect on many larger issues facing our time and the larger humanity. It is, metaphorically speaking, 'a collective prayer' by a large number of individuals who believe in the ideals of non-violence, fearlessness and love-force. The Dandi meeting is not a protest meeting. It is a meeting of minds for initiating constructive work and dialogue necessary for our time.
>
> Following the Dandi meet, Sarva-Bhasha-Samvad will continue to convene meetings and discussions for reflection, introspection and discussion in many towns and villages of several states from the 12th March to the 6th April—the duration of Mahatma Gandhi's Dandi march—in order to create a better understanding of the challenges facing us in the areas of creative expression and social harmony.

The announcement met with an enthusiastic response. I received mails from people in Assam, Punjab, Uttarakhand, Kerala, and Bengal, somewhat unexpectedly expressing their interest in participating in the Dandi dialogue, and a large number from Maharashtra, Goa, Gujarat, and Karnataka, too, wanted to join in.

In order to seek the necessary formal permission, Uttam Parmar, Surekha, and I visited Dandi. While discussing the proposed event with an elderly social activist, I was somewhat stunned when he remarked, 'Do whatever you like, but let not people who come here protest.' I was not stunned because *he* said it; I was stunned at the realisation that even Dandi, that most iconic stop in modern Indian history that has immortalised the Indian protest against the British, is probably no longer easily available to the present generation for even a peaceful *discussion* of protest. This is where Dandi is ninety-nine years after Mahadev Desai stepped into Gandhi's life. This is where Gujarat is, the state that in 2014 proposed a 'model' for the India of the future.

The Dakshinayan meeting at Dandi was attended by approximately 600 writers, drawn entirely voluntarily to it, from Maharashtra, Karnataka, Goa, Gujarat, Madhya Pradesh, Uttarakhand, Punjab, Assam, Kerala, and Bengal. Mahatma Gandhi's scholar-historian grandson Rajmohan was the main speaker. The young leaders of the ongoing struggle at the Indian Institute of Film Technology, Pune, were present, as were Hamid Dabholkar, Megha Pansare, and Sreevijay Kalburgi. Martin Macwan and several other dalit leaders, too, had joined us. All of them said, 'Let us be fearless.' Simple words, stated without any embellishment, they hit one hard. That day, Dakshinayan adopted Rabindranath Tagore's immortal line, 'Where the mind is without fear ...', as its motto.

The day after the Dandi meet, Surekha and I decided to leave Baroda for good and move to Dharwad to continue the Dakshinayan work. I knew that Mahatma Gandhi never returned to the Sabarmati Ashram after the Dandi march. His example was inspiring for me. During February 2016, we identified a house in Dharwad to rent for ourselves, and a few weeks later, we left Baroda for Dharwad, 1,000 km to the south, literally a *dakshinayan* for us.

For the next few months, a large number of intellectuals, social activists, and writers from various districts of Karnataka continued to visit me to express solidarity. Their numbers were so large and their backgrounds so enormously diverse that it soon became difficult for me to keep track of these visits. In order to make sense of the unexpected response springing up in Karnataka, I decided to seek the advice of a small but extremely perceptive group of friends in Dharwad. These included Shankar Halgatti, the General Secretary of the Karnataka Vidya Vardhak Sangh, M. D. Okkund and Vinaya Okkund, academics and poets, and Rajendra Poddar, a water activist and Professor of Agricultural Economics. There were others from various student unions, theatre groups, and publication houses. Soon, these consultative discussions acquired the shape of open meetings. We normally held these in the evenings at the Rangayana campus. For affairs pertaining to the entire state, I often consulted Rahmath Tarikere, who had returned his Akademi award, and Rajendra Chenni, an eminent literary critic. In June 2016, I convened a two-day meeting of some eighty key persons involved in Dakshinayan. The discussion brought forth the main issues troubling writers in many states—the rising trend of fascism, subversion of media autonomy, threats and intimidation that filmmakers and writers had to face, and shrinking of the space for free speech.

During the third week of June, I had to visit Grenoble in France for a conference. The news of Brexit came like a sharp pain while I was there. Others at the conference were also disturbed. In that agitated atmosphere, we sat talking about the changing world, and the views that came up in that discussion made it clear that democracies all over the world have a new challenge to face. I had been to Turkey for a lecture in 2014, soon after Tayyip Erdogan had been elected to power. A few months before that, I was in Egypt for a lecture at the American University campus; and in hushed voices, some of my Indian friends had narrated to me the stories of Abdel Fattah el Sisi's recent coup. The general atmosphere of fear was apparent for one to experience. In the year 2016, the possibility of Donald Trump being elected to the US Presidency loomed large, and in November that year, the fears came true. Thus, from 2013 to 2016, the Right was in ascendence everywhere in the world.

Back home in Dharwad, through the months of June–July, I spoke to small and big audiences about this change. I had to make frequent trips to Goa and Maharashtra to speak at literary and other public fora. I used these occasions to construct a meaning of the rapid transformation in the political atmosphere and its deep connection with the invasive information technology and deepening crisis in the international flow of capital. The weakened fabric of rational thought, the rise of theological orthodoxies, and the new slant in politics had a telling effect on democracies all over the world. India was no exception.

In 2016, 30 August marked a year of M. M. Kalburgi's murder. In memory of the slain scholar, the circle of friends that I had formed organised a silent walk in the streets of Dharwad. Many writers came to Dharwad from far-off places: Atamjit from Punjab, Siddharth Varadarajan, Chaman Lal, Githa Hariharan, and Antara Dev Sen from Delhi; Anand Patwardhan, Sanjiv Khadekar, and Anjum Rajbali from Bombay; a large number from Gujarat, Goa, and Maharashtra; several hundred from all parts of Karnataka; and quite a few thousand from Dharwad itself. The widows of the slain writers Narendra Dabholkar, Govind Pansare, and M. M. Kalburgi were present and flagged off the march. It ended in a large ground where a public meeting was to be held. Just as everyone arrived, a heavy downpour began. Everyone was drenched to the bone. I thought it would be proper to declare the meeting over and did so, but the audiences refused to move. They wanted to hear the scheduled speeches. The speakers spoke, and the audience of several thousand sat or stood as the rain kept pouring. I had not seen such commitment to the dignity of the word anywhere else in my four decades of literary life. The day after the Dharwad meeting, I received a call from the Home Minister of Karnataka, G. Parmeshwara. The meeting was convened to discuss the progress of investigations into the Kalburgi murder case. I thought it would be good to meet the minister with a group of Kannada writers. We met him in his office on 6 September. There were fourteen writers present and, after a ninety-minute discussion, the minister promised to ensure a speedy inquiry into the murder.

The Movement Spreads

The next large meeting of Dakshinayan was held at Madgaon in Goa in November 2016. It was attended by nearly 700 writers, mediapersons, thinkers, and theatre persons from Jammu and Kashmir, Punjab, West Bengal, Madhya Pradesh, Tamil Nadu, Kerala, Karnataka, Gujarat, Delhi, Rajasthan, and Telangana. The largest contingent came from Maharashtra. They travelled in buses, trains, cars, and on motorbikes. The meeting continued for three days and had fascinating lectures, discussions, and performances. Among the more notable thinkers present were Yogendra Yadav of the Swaraj India initative, TV journalists Rajdeep Sardesai, Sagarika Ghosh, and Nikhil Wagle, and philosophers Prakasha Shah from Gujarat and Raosaheb Kasbe from Maharashtra. The participants took out an evening march from the venue to the Lohiya Maidan, where they convened a large public meeting addressed by social activists and writers Uttam Parmar, Pradnya Daya Pawar, Megha Pansare, Hamid Dabholkar, Damodar Mauzo, and many others, including myself. The venue had a close symbolic link with the history of Goa's liberation struggle during the 1950s.

Thus, Dakshinayan once again expressed its commitment to the cause of freedom, this time the freedom of expression that a democracy must ensure. The Goa conference was hosted by Dakshinayan-Goa, very capably led by the Konkani writer Datta Naik and his close associates, Damodar Mauzo, Dilip Borkar,

Satyendra Sonar, and Dilip Sardesai. Many Christian writers participated in the conference, and so did large numbers of women. I was told by many in Goa that a convention of this kind had not been experienced earlier. The echoes of the Dakshinayan convention kept sounding in Goa for a long time. (That they impacted the Assembly elections some months later came as no surprise, but that is another story.) At the conclusion of the Goa convention, I announced that the next national Dakshinayan convention would be held at Nagpur. It was held on 30 January 2018.

Before I come to the Nagpur convention, I should describe, however sketchily, the numerous meetings, silent walks, publications, discussions, and initiatives that continued to be inspired by Dakshinayan. From the Dandi convention in January 2016 onwards, Vidya Bal from Pune, an octogenarian women's rights activist, had ensured a large participation of women writers at every meeting of Dakshinayan. Several issues of the movement journal that she and her colleague Geetali edit carried articles endorsing the writers' movement. A special number of *Sadhana*, a serious periodical with a subscriber base running into several thousand, was published. It contained pieces describing why writers had considered joining Dakshinayan and what they made of it. Although I was asked to be the guest editor, I decided not to write a long 'editorial piece' so as to not speak about the movement myself. This issue of *Sadhana* had a print run of several thousand copies more than usual, all of which were picked up eagerly. Several editorials also appeared from time to time in influential newspapers, hailing the Dakshinayan movement.

Writers involved in the movement regularly organised meetings of young artists, mediapersons, and social activists. At one such meeting held in Nashik in mid-2017, nearly 1,000 young persons participated. At Mangaon, known for its memorial to the legendary Marathi writer Sane Guruji, nearly 200 intellectuals gathered for three days to ponder on how to safeguard the freedom guaranteed in the Constitution. Advocate Prakash Ambedkar, grandson of the 'maker of the Indian Constitution', B. R. Ambedkar, was present and led the discussion. His wife Anjali Maydeo too was an active participant. Singers and artists from various parts of Maharashtra came together, inspired by renowned singer Shahir Sambhaji Bhagat, and formed a federation of artists under the name 'kala-jagar'. Painters and visual artists started coming together in Pune to celebrate the democratic and progressive spirit of medieval saint poets, as visible in the 'Wari'. This initiative was led by filmmaker and photographer Sandesh Bhandare.

In Karnataka, Rajendra Chenni held a large convention in Shimoga, with nearly 400 Kannada writers participating in it. Another was held in Dharwad to discuss the role of social media in protecting the freedom of expression. The most remarkable initiative emerged through my chance conversation with celebrated cinema artist Amol Palekar and his partner, Sandhya Gokhle. I asked them if they would select some films depicting resistance movements built around the principles of non-violence and courage. They did. The films they selected were screened in several cities by Dakshinayan writers. Sandhya made copies of the films and explained the logic behind her selection to every group. Nearly 30,000 viewers spread over thirty-five locations watched the nine stunningly well-made films selected by her over the next three months. She then offered a second lot, which was similarly watched. These included films from Kenya, Australia, Britain, America, and India. They provided Dakshinayan with an international element, driving home the point that the fight for freedom and justice is a universal undertaking.

A few months before the convention in Goa, I was to lecture at the 'Publishing Next' national publishers network conference in Kerala. One of the panels was on literature in translation. It was chaired by Mini Krishnan, who has led the translation programme of the Oxford University Press in India and, previously, that of Macmillan as well. At the end of the panel, I asked the audience if we could not put translation to the service of the freedom of expression. I proposed an informal after-dinner meeting, which was well-attended. I spoke briefly and suggested that in our dark times, it would be useful to compile anthologies of 'socially transformative literature' into various Indian languages, have them translated into English, and further re-translated into all other Indian languages. I was not sure how the publishers would respond, but to my delight, many showed an interest in the idea and volunteered to accept the anthologies for publication through their respective publishing houses. Ritu Menon, Vidya Rao, and Mini Krishnan, representing three eminent publishers, supported my idea that a 'consortium of publishers' be formed for this purpose, so that the onus did not fall on any single publisher to do something of this order.

In the weeks that followed, I mentioned this idea in my public lectures. The response to this was encouraging. At the Department of English and Cultural Studies, Ambedkar University Delhi, where I was to join a curriculum-forming workshop, the entire workshop turned into how these anthologies could be compiled. In that discussion, I found editors for the volumes in Urdu, Hindi, and Bengali. Elsewhere, I found scholars willing to edit such volumes in Marathi, Gujarati, Kannada, Malayalam, Punjabi, Telugu, Tamil, and Konkani. Thus, by the time the Dakshinayan writers met in Goa, I was prepared to announce the *Dakshinayan Indian Thought Series*. The series is designed to cover progressive moments in Indian thought traditions for over the past 1,000 years. By the time this book is published, publication of twelve of the proposed twenty-two volumes will be well underway. The Konkani volume, edited by Damodar Mauzo, is already published, and the Telugu volume edited by Volga and Kalpana Kannabiran, and the Punjabi volume edited by Atamjit Singh and H. K. Bhatia are just about to appear in print. These volumes come to approximately 5,000 printed pages. They bring together the very best of rational, progressive, and inspiring literature from some of the greatest writers in the past 1,000 years. Thus, by the end of 2017, the Dakshinayan movement had started expressing itself through literary publications, poems, theatre, cinema, special issues of magazines, public meetings, and youth activities. It had come to be a platform bringing together diverse thought and literary schools. It had opened a new horizon in times when the horizons of thought had started shrinking on all sides.

DAKSHINAYAN FOR THE FREEDOM OF EXPRESSION

The Nagpur meeting was very special, very important, for all of us. As part of the preparation, the local hosts, Pramod Munghate and Aruna Sabane, convened a number of meetings of socially committed writers and artists in Nagpur. They decided to involve a large number of colleges in the programme, and to invite writers to speak to the students there. In the initial list of colleges, they had over forty names. After scrutiny and involved discussions, this number was brought down to twenty-six.

While these preparations were on, students from various parts of Maharashtra assembled in Nasik. Madhav Palshikar took charge of the activities related to young persons. Looking at their enthusiasm, I thought of setting up a new kind of non-institutional Open University for them. The idea was welcomed. Towards this end, a number of meetings of thinkers and academics were held to see what kind of knowledge could be produced to bridge the gap between the formal university institutions and the lives lived by people outside them. Just as this thought was beginning to take root, a long essay of mine was published as a pocket book, under the title *The Crisis Within: Knowledge and Education in India*.[4] It was well-received. Many reviews and newspaper articles appeared about this work. It was translated into Marathi by Pramod Mujumdar and published later that year; K. P. Suresha translated it into Kannada, which was published in August 2018.

As all these activities continued, the month of August 2017 arrived and we started thinking about how the Kalburgi issue could be raised more effectively. I wrote to Chief Minister Siddaramaiah to draw his attention to the pending investigation into the murder. He promptly asked me to meet him. The meeting took place in Bangalore on 28 August. Surekha, Shankar Halgatti, Megha Pansare, and Rajendra Chenni accompanied me. We met at his residence as he was then recovering from a minor illness. He listened to us and promised that the investigation would soon be brought to a conclusion. I remember this meeting for an altogether different reason. As we emerged from the CM's house, we ran into Gauri Lankesh at the entrance of the bungalow. I had first met her in the mid-1990s at a village called Heggodu, where I had gone to meet the Kannada playwright Prasanna. She too had come to see him for a day. We had a long conversation, mostly in English, on many matters. At that time, she had not yet taken to activism; like any educated, middle-class Indian woman, she was at a remove from the toils and turmoils of life. Her father, the legendary P. Lankesh, was the cultural hero of Karnataka. In 2017, P. Lankesh was no more and Gauri was in the eye of every activist campaign in Karnataka. I asked her what she was doing at the residence of the CM, whom she knew quite well. She said she had come to ask him to expedite the Kalburgi murder investigation. Little did I know that the same killers were to assassinate her in less than a week!

Back in Dharwad, resting on the chief minister's assurance, we decided to hold just a simple public meeting and not a big silent march as in the previous year. The meeting was held at the Vidya Vardhak Sangh hall and attended by some 400 persons. Following that, we passed a resolution and sent it to the Karnataka government. Its text read:

> Resolution Passed in the Meeting organised by Dakshinayana's 'Dr. Kalburgi Hatya Virodhi Vedike' held on the 30th August 2017 at Vidya Vardhak Sangh, Dharwad, to demand Speedy Investigation in the case of Dr. M. M. Kalburgi, for submission to the Honourable Chief Minister of Karnataka.
>
> 'Dr. M. M. Kalburgi, an esteemed literary scholar, former Vice Chancellor of Hampi University, author of over 100 books, recipient of numerous awards, was shot dead two years ago in his residence in Kalyan Nagar of Dharwad.
>
> The murder was organized in a professional manner. The two assailants knocked the door of the residence of Dr. Kalburgi. Mrs. Umadevi Kalburgi opened the door. The assailants informed her that they are students of Dr. Kalburgi. She went inside to get coffee for them. By that time Dr. Kalburgi was also in the drawing room. At around 08.40 AM, one of the men fired two rounds at point blank range, striking Kalburgi's chest and forehead, while the other one waited outside keeping the motorcycle running. Immediately after the shooting, the assassins fled the scene on motorcycle. An ambulance was called and Dr. Kalburgi was taken to District Civil Hospital, Dharwad. Dr. Kalburgi was declared dead en route. Although a period of two years has elapsed since the tragedy, investigation by the State Police has not come to any conclusive end.
>
> After the death of Dr. Kalburgi, his daughter Mrs. R. S. Kinagi filed a police complaint at Vidyagiri Police Station of Dharwad, in which she categorically mentioned that she and her mother saw the two strangers who were responsible for the gruesome murder of her father and they can identify them. An F.I.R. No. 0142/2015 u/s 302 r/w 34 of I.P.C. and Section 25 of Arms Act was registered with Vidyagiri Police Station, Dharwad.

Dr. Narendra Dabholkar, who was spearheading agitation against superstition in the State of Maharashtra, was murdered in Pune on 20/08/2013 at 7.15 AM, by two motorcycle borne assailants, barely 500 meters from his residence, while on his morning walk.

Noted advocate and social activist Comrade Govind Pansare was shot along with his wife when they were taking morning walk on 16/02/2015. He succumbed to bullet injuries in Mumbai on 20/02/2015. It is pertinent to note that Comrade Pansare was an outspoken activist and was vocal against some of the cultural practices followed in the name of religion.

With a constant monitoring of investigation by High Court, C.B.I. arrested one Dr. Virendra Tawade in connection with murder of Late Dr. Dabholkar and even filed Charge-sheet against him in the Sessions Court, Pune. C.B.I. has identified Sarang Akolkar and Vinay Pawar as the shooters and even collected evidence about shooters. Out of the two Accused, Sarang Akolkar is an accused in Goa Bomb Blast case and is absconding since 2010. There is a red corner notice against him. The other person Vinay Pawar is also absconding after Goa Bomb Blast. C.B.I. is pursuing the shooters and Bombay High Court is still monitoring the investigation.

In the case of murder of Comrade Govind Pansare, Maharashtra Police also arrested one Sameer Gaikwad along with Dr. Virendra Tawade. Maharashtra Police have filed charge-sheets against the Accused. During the course of investigation of murder of Dr. Dabholkar and Comrade Pansare, there were meetings between officials of C.B.I., Maharashtra Police and Karnataka Police.

It is reported that bullets fired in all the three murders were sent for forensic analysis to ballistic experts. It appears that all three murders were committed by the same group of people and even weapons used in all three murders are same.

A special team of five inspectors headed by Assistant Commissioner of Police was formed by Hubli-Dharwad Police to investigate the murder of Dr. Kalburgi. Initial investigations revealed that the CCTV footage retrieved from the area show "two youths aged between 24 and 28, wearing black clothes and riding a motorcycle". Police also retrieved two empty cartridges from the crime scene and have said that an improvised firearm with 7.65 mm caliber bullets was used in the murder. On 03/09/2015 after four days from the murder of Dr. Kalburgi, Dharwad Police released sketches of the two suspects.

The investigation of the case of Dr. Kalburgi's assassination is being conducted by Karnataka C.I.D. During the investigation, Karnataka C.I.D., along with S.I.T. of Government of Maharashtra (that is investigating the murder of Comrade Govind Pansare) and C.B.I. (which is investigating the murder of Dr. Narendra Dabholkar), have found a clear nexus among all murders. However, till date there has been no conclusive statement by Karnataka C.I.D. in respect of involvement of the said accused in the murder of Dr. Kalburgi.

Dr. Kalburgi's murder, subsequent to the murders of Dr. Dabholkar and Comrade Govind Pansare, is a clear attack on the freedom of expression of thinkers and diversity of opinion.

Shocked by these gruesome serial murders of intellectuals, 39 writers from 14 states of India returned their awards received from the Sahitya Akademi, and 115 artists, film-makers and writers returned their awards received from other National and various State Academies. Artist and scientists from all parts of the country have expressed their concern over the atmosphere and intimidation prevailing in the country.

In response to representations from various delegations of citizens, writers and activists, Chief Minister of Karnataka Shri Siddramaiah had issued a statement expressing his full commitment to speedily bringing the investigation in the case of Dr. Kalburgi's murder to its conclusion and bringing the culprits to book.

On this 30th August 2017, two years from the day of the tragic assassination of one of Karnataka's most gifted scholars and thinkers, we wish to convey our utmost anxiety and pain about the slow speed of investigation. We urge the Honourable Chief Minister to bring the investigation to its logical conclusion with the utmost sense of urgency.

We would like to point out that allowing the fascistic tendency of elimination of diversity of thought and attacking thinkers should have no place in Karnataka. It is a state where literature and arts have flourished over the centuries. We urge the Government of Karnataka to ensure that the atmosphere of fear caused by the murder of Dr. Kalburgi be dispelled by speedy action. Words will mean more when they are matched with action.

We demand:

1. A meeting of our representatives with the Highest Officers of the CID and Home Ministry of the Government of Karnataka to discuss the gaps in the investigation
2. Closer collaboration among the three investigating agencies and the three states involved in the enquiry of the three linked murders of intellectuals
3. Bringing the investigation to a logical conclusion within a period of the next three to four months.'

Signed by Rajendra Chenni, Dhanaji Gurav, G. N. Devy, Surekha Devi, Shankar Halgatti, Sanjeev Kulkarni, A. M. Khan, B. N. Pujar, M. D. Okkund, K. H. Patil.

After we sent the resolution to the government, I was called by the CID police department of the Karnataka government to discuss the progress in the investigation. I met them in Bangalore on 2 September. They assured me that they had been keeping a close eye on the movements of the suspected assassins. Rajendra Chenni, Surekha, and I returned from the meeting, hopeful that the end of the investigations was in sight. Exactly seventy-two hours later, I learnt of Gauri Lankesh's assassination from 'breaking news' on television. We instantly rushed to the Ambedkar Statue at the Basava Circle. Within minutes, a number of activist-friends had gathered, as did those whom I did not know. Strangers, young persons, women, men, many gathered there. Some brought with them pictures of Gauri, downloaded from mobiles and printed out hastily. There was anger, grief, and shock in the air. One felt as if one had been gagged and was being dragged to a death chamber. The next morning, I wrote the following article in *The Wire*, the complete text of which is given below:[5]

On the day of Ganesh visarjan, Gauri is gone.

The last I met her was a week back.

That was at the entrance of the residence of the chief minister of Karnataka.

I had gone there with the literary critic and activist Rajendra Chenni to express our anguish over the delay in the investigation into the M.M. Kalburgi assassination case.

As I was stepping out of chief minister Siddaramaiah's house, I ran into her. She had come there to do precisely the same.

The fearless crusader who was talking last week to the CM of Karnataka about speeding up the Kalburgi murder investigation was assassinated last evening.

Exactly as Narendra Dabholkar, Comrade Govind Pansare and Dr. Kalburgi were assassinated in 2013 and 2016.

In her case, as in the earlier three killings, motor-cycle borne assailants were deployed, who fired at point blank distance, and then fled.

Reports say seven bullets were fired. Three weapons were used. Three persons committed the cold-blooded, carefully premeditated murder.

Three men, three weapons, seven bullets and a 55-year-old frail, tired, single woman.

Had William Blake been alive, he would have said in agony,

"What immortal hand or eye

Could frame thy fearful symmetry?"

However, the fearful symmetry of conspiracy cannot intimidate fearless and spirited voices like Gauri's.

Throughout her career as a journalist, she spoke out relentlessly, without a shred of fear, against oppression and injustice.

Even when she had to face imprisonment for her views, face isolation among activists due to her distinct way of thinking, face intimidation due to controversies arising out of her actions, she remained committed to her cause. And what was her cause? That of every self-respecting media person in the world—of placing reality as it is in public view.

Some minutes past 8 pm on Tuesday evening, the news of Gauri's assassination started coming. It spread from TV channels to mobiles like a wildfire.

By 9 pm, journalists in Bangalore, Dharwad, Gulbarga, Shimoga and many other cities in Karnataka had gathered in public places. They spoke. They took out candle-lit processions.

During the night, they took buses and trains to reach Bangalore where a meeting began at 10 am in the city's town hall. It may continue well past the sunset.

In Dharwad, where I moved to live since Dr. Kalburgi's assassination, media persons, writers, activists and students started assembling in the morning itself. We have issued a request for colleges and universities in Dharwad to remain closed for the day. Was it not Teacher's Day when Gauri was shot dead?

We will then walk in a silent rally to the centre of town. Later in the day, I plan to drive to Pune, 450 kms north of Dharwad, where journalists have called for a meeting to mourn the assassination. Many of them had never met Gauri personally. But they shudder at the kind of onslaught let loose on the media. Is the media not a centrally vital organ of democracy? That is precisely why so many journalists believe that democracy today is under a siege.

Most of us have spent a sleepless night. Late in the night or early in the morning, it is difficult for me to recall exactly when,

Rajmohan Gandhi sent a mail from across the seas. His message combined his sense of shock and outrage at the murder and the concern for personal safety of some of us who have been vocal.

Twenty months ago, when we met at Dandi—nearly 700 writers, artists and activists had gathered to protest the third assassination, that of Kalburgi—Rajmohan Gandhi gave a very brief speech. All that he said was that Gandhi learnt how to be fearless from Kasturba. "Be fearless," he said, "That is the only way to fight Fascism."

Gauri has taught us once again how to be fearless. Let us have the Mahatma's humility to learn it from her.

Times are strange, and they can get stranger still.

Over the next few days, the killing of Gauri Lankesh occupied the nation's attention. On 12 September, a huge procession was taken out in Bangalore to mourn Gauri, which culminated in a meeting. It was attended by over 30,000 people. Speakers had come from all parts of the country, and all bemoaned the fact that free speech had come under such brutal assault. Gauri died in the attack, but the flame of resistance that she lit in millions of hearts kept burning for a long time.

It was against this background that the Nagpur convention of Dakshinayan was held on 29–30 January 2018. The venue for the meeting on the 29th was the Sevagram Ashram, the place where Mahatma Gandhi had stayed after leaving the Sabarmati Ashram in 1931 and walking to Dandi. Inside the hall and outside it, there were close to 600 people. I requested every speaker to speak in her/his mother tongue. A total of eleven languages were used at the meeting. In all those languages, the speakers articulated how they had responded to the killing of Gauri Lankesh. It was a multilingual tribute to courage. I shall never forget the serenity and the unbreakable resolve that filled the air. I do not think anyone present there that evening can forget it.

The next morning, after prayers at the ground where Gandhi used to pray, we assembled to listen to Prakash Ambedkar and Rajmohan Gandhi. For decades, the followers of Gandhi and Ambedkar have not seen eye to eye. There has been great animosity and mutual suspicion between them. The coming together of the two grandsons of the two great persons who charted the destiny of India was an experience that country has not had since Independence. Hundreds of people came to listen to them, from far distances. I made a short concluding speech and announced my idea to set up a new kind of open 'non-institution'. When the meeting was concluded, I requested Ambedkar and Gandhi to accompany me to Bapu Kutir, the little cottage in which Gandhi lived while at Sevagram. When they, Ishaan, Rashmi, and I were in the cottage, I asked the two of them to be the honorary Chancellors of the new 'multi-varsity'. They agreed. We were all silent, for quite a while.

Later, all of the Dakshinayan colleagues left for Nagpur, an hour and a half away from Wardha. That morning in Wardha, nearly 160 writers had already visited the colleges assigned to them and spoken to the students and faculty. All of them—students, faculty, and people present at Wardha in the morning—assembled at the Dikshabhumi, known as the sacred place where Babasaheb Ambedkar had embraced Buddhism seventy years ago. A few of us were taken to visit the urn carrying his ashes. The thousands present there took out a procession leading to the Dhanavate National College, headed by the extremely brave Principal Taywade. A public meeting took place here. Apart from Prakash Ambedkar and Rajmohan Gandhi, the speakers included Medha Patkar, Raosaheb Kasbe, K. K. Chakravarty, and Dhanaji Gurav. The meeting was followed by an inspiring Shahiri concert by Sambhaji Bhagat. What an experience that was! A former Secretary to the Government of India, Vibha Puri Das, was present with us throughout the two days. Writing to her civil services colleagues several months later, she recalled:

> Nagpur [30 January 2018] saw the coalescing of the energies and forces of Gandhian thought, Ambedkar activism, progressive morchas of a range of litterateurs, cultural ambassadors, artistes, teachers and students. Twenty private colleges and their managements came forward to lend their infrastructure, premises and their energies to hosting this conclave and the discussion, meeting culminating in an energising music programme with satire, humour and foot tapping rhythms. A galaxy of speakers led by Rajmohan Gandhi and Prakash Ambedkar in putting the government on notice that vitiation of the spirit of the constitution will not be tolerated. Earlier, while offering tributes to Gauri Lankesh, young voices had celebrated that for last Fourty [*sic*] years (since the emergency) progressive forces have been quarreling amongst themselves. First time that they have come together. The *urja,* as most speakers declared emphatically, for this came from Ganesh Devy. Ganesh Devy has been the glue to bring disparate forces in sync, provide a conceptual understanding of the nature of the authoritarian edifice we confront and reveal the true face of the fascism we encounter in language and idiom acceptable to a vast variety of intellectuals and youth while powering a singularly creative counter to it and continue the fight for greater space for constitutionalism.[6]

UNDERSTANDING DAKSHINAYANA

It is not as if, while Dakshinayan was taking shape as a movement, nothing else of significance was taking place in the country. Although, in October 2015, there were few or none at all who had the courage to speak up, by the beginning of 2018 numerous informal groups had sprung up in different parts of the country. The media, unfortunately, no longer carries news about such groups, as it used to do in the past. But this does not mean that such groups do not exist. On the other side, repression and intimidation continued; the film *Padmavat*, depicting a fictionalised episode in the history of Rajasthan, was blocked for a while, mainly in the BJP-ruled states. Some mediapersons in Assam and UP were killed in broad daylight, others were threatened with imprisonment or sedition. NDTV, a major news channel, was slapped with a day's symbolic closure.[7] The Ministry of Information and Broadcasting issued a circular to announce punitive measures for 'fake' news, which was later withdrawn in the face of sharp criticism.[8]

Meanwhile cow vigilantes continued to crisscross the plains of central India in search of innocent victims; Hindu girls married to Muslim men (termed 'love jihad') were compelled to 'return home'; and '*ghar wapsi*', or 'returning home' became the term used for coerced reconversion activities, in which non-Hindus were forced to become Hindus. Individuals were killed by mobs on mere suspicion of their having eaten or stored beef.[9] Anyone who dared criticise the prime minister was branded 'anti-national'. Members of the Scheduled Caste were beaten and humiliated in public at a place like Una in Gujarat.[10] University students were targeted if they expressed any non-conformist views, and Rohith Vemula of Hyderabad Central University was driven to commit suicide in desperation.[11] High Court judges were driven to recuse themselves from cases involving criminal proceedings against high-placed political leaders, and one such judge later died under suspicious circumstances.[12]

Everyone with an independent view was trolled through organised social media, and even a former prime minister, who had dinner with a Pakistani diplomat, was described as a 'traitor'.[13] An eminent editor of a Kashmiri newspaper was murdered during festival days,[14] and an 80-year-old Hindu monk activist was beaten up by young goons.[15] And while all this became a routine matter, protests and scattered resistance continued to spring up in different cities and rural areas. The protesters and their informal groups evolved an unstated principle of mutual collaboration across affiliations, focus-interests, and their specific constituencies. This was a widespread strife, with a logic and grammar of its own, previously unknown in India.

In line with that grammar and logic, Dakshinayan chose to remain a process and did not attempt to become an organisation. It has not been affiliated to any political party, nor does it aspire to float any party. It is a process aimed at bringing together conscientious and courageous individuals who respect the Constitution and the principles of diversity, justice, and democracy enshrined in it. Ever since the process was initiated in August 2015 at Baroda, it has continued to be dynamic. Through a series of events, discussions, protest meetings, publications, consultations, and regional or national conferences, it has been gaining greater momentum.

There have been literary movements in India in the past. These include not only the movements within literature that gave rise to new genres, trends, styles, and themes, but also movements focused on social and cultural issues. During the Indian freedom struggle, writers actively participated in anti-British activities. During the period of transition from British rule to Independence, the Progressive Writers and Indian People's Theatre Association (IPTA) sided with the poor and downtrodden social classes. Karl Marx shaped their political discourse and Berthold Brecht their theatre expression. The contribution of those movements to Indian literature, theatre, and cinema has been significant. Yet, Dakshinayan has been markedly different from those previous movements: the two former movements sprang up in response to the rift between the West and the East in post-war global politics. The Indian government of the day was avowedly socialist in nature, and the writers did not have to court its wrath. Rather, they appeared to be the frontrunners of an ideology that the country had already accepted.

Later, an extremely powerful and pervasive dalit literary movement emerged in India during the 1960s and 1970s. It hit out against the oppressive caste discrimination, and continues to dominate the social imagination of most Indian writers. The presiding deity of dalit literature was Babasaheb Ambedkar. He continues to inspire dalit writers even today. And, indeed, caste discrimination still haunts Indian society, perhaps more severely than before.

The Dakshinayan movement is different from these movements in that, while it is explicitly anti-caste and anti-communal, it is not primarily engaged in these issues. Its focus is the idea of the freedom of expression. The earlier movements were constructed round the question of justice—social and political—with regard to caste, class, and gender. Dakshinayan is an anti-fascist movement, focused primarily on the question of the freedom of speech, thought, and expression. In that sense, it is without cognisable precedence in India. However, if one were to look for any underpinning thought driving Dakshinayan, one would have to name Mahatma Gandhi and the legacy of his ideas of truth and non-violence. The choice of locations for two of the large conventions of Dakshinayan—Dandi and Wardha—clearly point to how much Dakshinayan draws from Gandhi. Rabindranath Tagore's immortal line, 'where the mind is without fear', and Gandhi's message of fearlessness constitute Dakshinayan's core values.

Sometime in September 2017, I received a call from London asking me if I would consider convening the PEN International Congress for 2018 in India. I was aware that PEN—initially an acronym for Poets, Essayists, and Novelists—is an organisation with a long history, and that it works for freedom of speech. Therefore,

I expressed my consent. The Director of PEN International asked me to go to Ukraine, where the 2017 PEN Congress was to meet. I did so. Our discussion about the possibility of holding the next PEN Congress in India continued. After considering various venues, I proposed that it be held in Pune. My reason was simple. This is where Gandhi and Kasturba Gandhi had been kept in jail (not their first jail term, though), when Kasturba breathed her last. It was Kasturba who transformed Gandhi's *satyagraha* struggle in South Africa before they returned to India and vitalised the Indian freedom struggle. I thought it important to bring writers from all the countries in the world to pay a fresh homage to her in her place of eternal rest at the Aga Khan palace in Pune. It was also here that Narayan Desai's father and Gandhi's secretary for almost a quarter of a century, Mahadev Desai, died. If this were to happen when the world celebrates the 150th year of Gandhi's birth (1869) from 2 October 2018, it would be the most appropriate way to spread the message of fearlessness. The PEN International enthusiastically agreed to my suggestion.

As a result, major writers from nearly eighty countries congregated in Pune in the last week of September 2018. Together with the writers involved in Dakshinayan, they walked up to the Aga Khan palace and spent some time in complete silence. Later in the week, they joined in a *wari*, a literary pilgrimage tradition in existence in Maharashtra for over a millennium, carrying signboards for nearly 6,000 languages of the world. This was to be our tribute to the human voice and speech, which is what makes us human. That *wari* on the eve of Gandhi's 150th birth anniversary was Dakshinayan's appeal to the world that speech needs to be protected, its assertion that freedom and voice matter. We owe it to all writers and thinkers who were killed for what they wrote or thought, to all those who sacrificed their lives so that we could have the freedom to speak and think without fear of intimidation.

Notes and References

1. Unpublished text, to be included in an anthology of essays by the movement members on the Dakshinayana movement.

2. Available at Parliament of India, Lok Sabha, https://loksabha.nic.in.

3. Ibid.

4. G. N. Devy, *The Crisis Within: Knowledge and Education in India* (New Delhi: Aleph, 2017).

5. G. N. Devy, 'Gauri Lankesh has Taught us Once Again How to be Fearless', *The Wire*, 6 September 2017. Reproduced here with permission from *The Wire*.

6. In an e-mail sent to a group of former bureaucrats, copied to me.

7. Himanshi Dhawan, 'Government's blackout of two TV news channels dangerous for democracy', *The Times of India*, 7 November 2016. Available at https://timesofindia.indiatimes.com/india/Governments-blackout-of-two-TV-news-channels-dangerous-for-democracy/articleshow/55282622.cms (accessed April 2019).

8. 'Ministry withdraws order on "fake news"', *The Hindu*, 4 April 2018. Available at https://www.thehindu.com/news/national/ministry-withdraws-order-on-fake-news/article23428180.ece (accessed April 2019).

9. Chapal Mehra, 'The who, what and where of Dadri', *The Hindu*, 24 March 2016. Available at https://www.thehindu.com/opinion/open-page/dadri-lynching-incident-the-who-what-and-where-of-dadri/article7754192.ece (accessed April 2019).

10. 'Gujarat: 7 of Dalit family beaten up for skinning dead cow', *The Indian Express*, 20 July 2016. Available at https://indianexpress.com/article/india/india-news-india/gujarat-7-of-dalit-family-beaten-up-for-skinning-dead-cow-2910054/ (accessed April 2019).

11. Omer Farooq, 'Rohith Vemula: The student who died for Dalit rights', *BBC News*, 19 January 2016. Available at https://www.bbc.com/news/world-asia-india-35349790 (accessed April 2016).

12. 'Death of a Judge: What We Know, What We Don't Know', *The Wire*, 12 January 2018. Available at https://thewire.in/politics/judge-loya-death-questions (accessed April 2019).

13. PTI, 'Manmohan Singh defied national line by meeting Pakistan diplomats: Arun Jaitley', *Hindustan Times*, 11 December 2017. Available at https://www.hindustantimes.com/assembly-elections/jaitley-rules-out-pm-apology-for-targeting-manmohan/story-lPnP2DAafBfqFCrbXlbnhI.html (accessed April 2019).

14. PTI (Srinagar), 'Rising Kashmir editor Shujaat Bukhari shot dead in Srinagar', *Hindu Business Line*, 14 June 2018. Available at https://www.thehindubusinessline.com/news/rising-kashmir-editor-shujaat-bukhari-shot-dead-in-srinagar/article24165181.ece (accessed April 2019).

15. Amarnath Tewary, 'Swami Agnivesh beaten up by BYJM workers in Jharkhand', *The Hindu*, 17 July 2018. Available at https://www.thehindu.com/news/national/other-states/swami-agnivesh-beaten-up-by-bjym-workers-in-jharkhand/article24442985.ece (accessed April 2019).

POSTSCRIPT

When historical narratives become semantic beggars, anecdotes help in lighting up collective memory. Some years ago, I was in Berlin. This was the post-perestroika, unified Berlin. As I was walking outside the grand buildings of Berlin University, where Karl Marx had been a student a century and a half ago, I noticed a curious installation just outside the university library. It was designed to take one by complete surprise and shock. On the pavement, as one walked, one suddenly saw a small cavity covered in glass. It was the size of a cellar, or a war-field bunker. Inside, there was some light, which was, however, not bright enough to illuminate its contents immediately. As one peered into the dimly lit room under the glass roof, one noticed a single shelf, with no books on it. There were perhaps just one or two books on the shelf, lying as if lifeless. The inscription placed beside the glass surface read, 'This is the place where Adolf Hitler burnt books of many thinkers in May 1932 after dragging them out of the library.' The inscription brought home the brutality of the regime that took pride in attacking free thought. The installation was an apt statement of the tradition of Marx, brutalised by Hitler.

That eloquent installation has remained in my memory as an unforgettable experience. It suddenly surfaced again when, recently, I walked past a similar installation. This time, it was in Michigan, a bastion of free thought, fighting to preserve its identity in the present regime in the United States. This installation, created by a little-known Luzinterruptus arts-collective in Spain, was made up of 10,000 books spread on Liberty Street. They were open, as if someone had been reading them, but was only half-way through. Many of them were children's stories, some were about text and design, and some were traveller's tales. But the larger bulk included books of philosophy. The inscription placed on one side said, 'You are welcome to walk over these books, take them away and do what you like with them.'[1] For any book lover, the scene was painful. It brought home with utmost clarity the fact that the phrase 'post-truth' means an utter contempt for ideas.

A day after I had passed by the installation in Michigan, American TV channels were reporting on how pipe bombs had been delivered to the CNN office and the residences of Barack Obama and Hillary Clinton. The analysts were unanimous in claiming that this was a moment that the entire nation must condemn the incidents in one voice, and a joint communiqué needed to be issued to warn those who had dispatched those lethal bombs. They also pointed out that it was probably President Donald Trump's tirade against the Democrats that had emboldened the perpetrator to use such violent devices. One expected some shade of remorse in Trump's statement on the horrifying incident; however, when he actually spoke, there was none. Rather, in the tone of a scolding schoolteacher, he reprimanded Obama and Clinton, 'No one should carelessly compare political opponents to historical villains, which is done often, it's done all the time, got to stop.'[2] This was much like the characteristic response to violence in India.

While capitalism had many ills, it also had a certain ethical decorum. However, the post-truth political regimes have stripped capitalism bare by casting aside even the pretence of capitalistic democracy being based on consent and dialogue. Criticism and questioning have become bad words in the post-truth crony capitalism of political regimes in many parts of the world. No wonder, then, that books are now to be trampled upon.

A related anecdote that comes to mind concerns the Kasturba memorial in the Aga Khan palace in Pune. Kasturba Gandhi died here during her imprisonment; she, Gandhi, and Mahadev Deasai had been imprisoned here at the height of World War II and the Quit India movement. Recently, as mentioned in Chapter 3, I had the privilege of hosting the PEN International conference in Pune at which writers from eighty-seven countries participated. I thought it would be a good idea to bring the writers to the Kasturba memorial, which I did. I had imagined that these writers from far-off countries would look at the place, take a few photographs, and then want to leave. To my surprise, they stated that they would like to sit on the ground and observe silence as a tribute to Gandhi and Kasturba. The genuine respect and love that they inspire even amongst those who are complete strangers to their work and ideas is phenomenal.

Although Hitler was younger than Gandhi by some twenty years, the two can be seen as contemporaries dominating the world stage. It was at approximately the same time that Hitler had books burnt in Berlin and Gandhi defied the colonial salt law and chose to be jailed. Around the same time that Gandhi came up with his idea of 'civil disobedience' as a statement of one's moral courage in the face of injustice, Hitler began demanding 'complete obedience' towards the supreme leader. Hitler justified and promoted violence in every form, Gandhi devoted himself to preaching non-violence. Hitler made propaganda the basis of his continued right to dominate, and Gandhi spoke of truth as the path towards freedom.

It is an irony of history that the world is celebrating the 150th year of Gandhi's birth, 2018–19, precisely when the tendencies for which Hitler was known have started characterising rulers in many countries. Was Gandhi's idea of truth so fragile that the world could forsake it not long after his death? The writers gathered in Pune brought home to me poignantly that Gandhi is still seen by the larger humanity, irrespective of one's nation, creed, language, and race, as the prophet of freedom. He returns to people's thought wherever love, freedom, and truth are assailed. The post-truth era in history will no doubt make him sound as relevant as he was in the times of colonialism and Hitler's festival of violence. No installation will make him look dated and embarrassing, not even the ridiculous official caricature of him as only a pair of glasses, used to promote the ideas of those who despise him.

Unfettered greed has resulted in limitless violence. Our caste hatred, class conflicts, gender relations, racial inequalities, religious fundamentalism, media deterioration, and obsession with self-glorification, all go to show how internalised violence has become to our thought, speech, and existence. Yet conscience, which Shakespeare once stated 'makes cowards of us all', can free us from it, at least in some measure. Every individual, wherever they are, can try to be fearless and selfless, can say 'no' to intimidation and terror, to greed and self-obsession. My conclusion may be easily dismissed as naïve and simplistic. The three chapters in the book are presented to show that if we analyse the source of violence, observe carefully the violence surrounding us, and act to counter it through the fearless articulation of truth, it may become possible to take humans beyond violence, despite whatever the past of the species might be.

NOTES AND REFERENCES

1. Ben Allan Smith, '10,000 books put on display on Liberty Street in Ann Arbor', *MLive Michigan*, 24 October 2018. Available at https://expo.mlive.com/news/erry-2018/10/9a7f06203d5635/10000-books-put-on-display-on.html (accessed April 2019).

2. John Swaine and David Smith, 'Suspected bombs sent to prominent Trump critics "an act of terror"', *The Guardian*, 25 October 2018. Available at https://www.theguardian.com/us-news/2018/oct/24/clinton-bomb-reports-delivery-home-new-york-hillary-bill-latest (accessed April 2019).

INDEX

Aaj Kaal 66
Act of violence 30, 32
Adivasi Academy of Tejgadh 108, 110
Adivasi communities xvi, 108
  atrocities on 43
Aesthetics of conflict 38
After Amnesia (1992) 93
Agricultural income 80
Agricultural labour 81
Ambedkar, B. R. 119, 130, 134
Ambedkar, Prakash 119, 130
Andha-shraddha Nirmulan Samiti (ANIS) 102
Animals, killing of 15
Anthropology 16, 31
Arendt, Hannah 5–6
Arjuna–Krishna dialogue, on philosophy of violence and death 17–19, 21
Artificial intelligence x
Aurobindo; *see* Ghosh, Aurobindo
Award returning phenomenon 95–96, 125
  Government's request to take back the awards 96
  list of the writers who had returned their awards 97–98
  Parliament response toward 96–99
Award-wapasi; see award returning phenomenon

Babari Masjid, demolition of (1992) xii
Bank operations, in tribal areas 75
Bengal, partition of (1905) 29
Bhagawad Gita 17–18, 50–51
  Arjuna–Krishna dialogue 17–19
  Aurobindo's *Essays on the Gita* 20, 50
  concept of
    nivrutti 50
    pravrutti 50
    sthitapragnya 50
  Gandhi translation of 50
  Jnanadev's commentary on 50
  karmamarga, concept of 51
  philosophy of control over the senses 22
  significance of 20
  teachings on philosophy of action 20
  Tilak's *Gita Rahasya* 20, 50

Bhaktimarga, concept of 52–53
Bhandare, Sandesh 102, 119
Bharatiya Janata Party (BJP) 77, 96
Bhave, Vinoba 106, 112
Bhil community
  menace of the denotified Bhils 80
  notification during British rule 80
Bhoodan movement 106
Blake, William 38, 56
Brexit 115
Bride burning 23, 43–44; *see also* *Sati,* practice of
Bride-price 82
British rule 29, 47, 80, 133
  parliamentary democracy 40

Calcium Fluoride (fluorspar) mining 81
Capitalism x, 15, 38, 139
Capitalist economy 45
Capitalistic democracy 139
Caste–class-ridden society xii
Caste strife 23
Chemistry of violence 3–4, 31
Chenni, Rajendra 91, 115, 119, 122, 126, 127
Chhota Udepur 61, 67
  foodgrain banks in 86
  timber merchants at 80
  tribal population of 68
  tribal riots in 67
  Tribal sub-plan in 65
  weekly *haat* 65
Childhood; *see also* School children, in India
  and adolescence 35, 37
  destruction in the name of education 38
Christianity
  Christian theology 16
  and fear of death 16
Civil disobedience, idea of 140
Civil society 14
Class conflicts 141
Colonisation ix, 16
Committee for Eradication of Superstitions; *see* Andha-shraddha Nirmulan Samiti (ANIS)
Commodification of violence 28
Communal politics 69
Communal riots xii
  in Chhota Udepur 67
  Godhra incident 61, 70
  in Gujarat xv–xvi, 68–69
  in Panvad village 63–64
  in Tejgadh village 61–63, 72
Communism 49
Concentration camps xv, 3
Consciousness, philosophy of 9, 11, 19–20, 26–27
Constitution of India
  Article 5 (2,6) of the Fifth Schedule 78
Control over the senses, philosophy of 22
Countering violence, method for 46–53

creation of desire and 47
Gandhi's method of non-violence 47, 49–50
by industrialisation 48
legal punishment 46–47
by material acquisition 49
by spiritual force 49
by teachings of Bhagawad Gita 50
by technological development 48
Creative expression, freedom of 89, 113
Creativity, sense of 30–31, 39
Crime in society
crime–politics nexus xii
incidence of 4, 33
and punishment 4, 8, 23
Criminality
criminal tendencies and 3–4, 6, 10, 23, 25, 27, 30, 32
law and punitive measures 8
as a social perversity 8
Criminal law 8, 25
Criminals 4, 9–10, 39, 45
Criminal Tribes Act (1871) 80
Criminal violence 7
Criminology
objective of 4
prime purpose of 4
Cross-border terrorism 68
Cultural
acceptability 24
cynicism 36
factors 2
nationalism 111
personality 41
practice 24, 45, 124
prakruti (selfhood) 42

Dabholkar, Narendra 91, 99, 101–04, 114, 116, 124–25, 127
Dakshinayan Indian Thought Series 120
Dakshinayan movement xvii, 89
as anti-fascist movement 134
attack on a folk singer 100–101
award returning phenomenon 95–96
Parliament response toward 96–99
'*Chalo* Dandi' 105, 106–17
Dandi convention 114, 118
for freedom of creative expression 89
for freedom of expression 121–31
Goa conference 117–18
Kalburgi, killing of 90–95
Nagpur convention 118, 121, 129
spread of 117–21
understanding of 101–5, 131–35
writers' discontent and 95–96
writers involved in 118
Dalits 23, 45–46, 59, 112, 114, 134
Daruwalla, Keki N. 97, 99
Deasai, Mahadev 106, 140
Death, fear of 15–22
capitalist society's 16
Christian theology on 16

Indian philosophy on 17
main cause of 15
as natural event 17
old age and 15
philosophy of 17
surgical operations and 16
in Western medical science 16
Western philosophy on 15–16
Decision-making
infiltration of criminals into 39
political 39
Deforestation, in Panvad village
ecological dangers of 80
by timber merchants 80
Democracy 40, 42, 99–101, 117, 128, 133, 139
Denotified tribals, situation of 80, 86
Depression 24, 58
Desai, Narayan 106, 107, 112
Desire, creation of 47
Detachment, spirit of 19, 50
Devi, Mahasweta xii, 79, 85, 86, 107, 108–10
Devotion 20, 43, 51–53
Devy, Ganesh 104–5, 131
Dharma, notion of 18, 21, 48
Dignity of labour 48
Disillusionment, sense of 42
Distanced violence
concept of 28–34
indicators of 28
infliction of pain and suffering 28
Dreyfus case 5–6
Drug trafficking 39, 81
Durkheim, Emile 7–10, 30
Ecology
needs of 48
of thought ix
Economic empowerment, of tribals 76
Economic perspective of criminal violence 7
Education system in India
to address spiritual and creative potential in the child 38
under British colonial rule 38
resources for funding 39
tendency towards violence 38
Vora Committee Report on 39
Elected representatives of people 40, 76
Emergency of India (June 1975–March 1977) xi, xii, 93
Employment 12, 36–38, 61, 67, 80–81
Energism (*pravritti*) 20
Enlightenment, philosophy of 19, 47
Ethics xv, 4, 53
Ethnic and caste identity politics xii
Ethos of violence 36
Expression, freedom of 104–5, 117
Dakshinayan movement for 121–31
protest against the attack on 105
role of social media in protecting 119

'Fake' news, punitive measures for 132
Fantasy, world of 4, 11, 13–14, 22

Fascism, horrors of xv, 103, 112, 115, 129, 131
Fear, emotion of 15
Femininity 41, 43, 47
Folk singer, attack on 100–01
Foodgrains bank scheme 85–86
Forest Kamdar Sangh 80
Freedom struggle 39, 133, 135
French Revolution (1789–99) 6, 29

Galileo 9, 10, 47
Gandhi, Indira 91
Gandhi, Kasturba xvii, 129, 135, 140
Gandhi Katha 109
Gandhi, Mahatama 45, 47, 52, 106, 129, 135, 140
  assassination of xi, 91
  birth anniversary of xvii
  civil disobedience, idea of 140
  comparison with Hitler 140
  Dandi march 113
  on driving the British out of India 40
  Hind Swaraj 34, 40
  notion of non-violence x
  opposition to
    British colonial masculinity 47
    colonial salt law 140
  on parliamentary form of government 40
  satyagraha 47, 135
  translation of Bhagawad Gita 50
  truth, idea of 140
Gandhi, Rajiv 91
Gandhi, Rajmohan 114, 129–31
Gender discrimination 43, 46
Genetic disorder 4, 37
Genocides 32–33
  attacks on Sikhs (1984) xii
Geographical conditions 1
Germany Nazi violence 5
  Holocaust xv
Ghar wapsi 132
Ghosh, Aurobindo 21, 34
  Essays on the Gita 20, 50
  philosophy of evolution from matter to mind 51
  understanding of the Gita 51
God, concept of 2
  as a passive agency 49
Godhra incident 61, 70
Gokhle, Sandhya 119
Government of India 96, 130
Greed ix–x, xviii, 18, 35, 43, 45, 47, 49, 141
'Green' revolution xii
Gujarat Mineral Development Corporation (GMDC) 81
Gujarat *Samachar* 85
Gupta, Dipankar 66
Guruji, Sane 102, 118

Haats 65, 76, 87
Halgatti, Shankar 115, 122, 126
Haridaspur 57–58, 60, 69–70, 84
Hind Swaraj 34, 40
Hindu fundamentalism 67
Hindu sectarian movements 64
Hindutva 68, 70, 73, 81

Hitler, Adolf 33, 138, 140
anti-Jewish propaganda 6
belief in the glory of untruth 14
childhood of 12
comparison with Gandhi 140
festival of violence 141
in German army 12
hatred for the human species 12
imprisoned in Landresburg prison 13
Mein Kampf 13
Munich Beer Hall revolt 13
National Socialist (Nazi) party 12
philosophy of violence 13–15
political career 12
political philosophy of 13
Holocaust xv
Human
consciousness 20
freedom 16
greed ix–x, xviii, 18, 35, 43, 45, 47, 49, 141
psyche 34, 41–42, 45, 47, 83
sacrifices 8, 23
volition 32

Ideology of progress 48
Impotence, fear of 10–11, 14–15, 18, 33
Indian cinema, violence in xii
scale and degree of 36
Indian culture, notions of violence in 17, 19, 42, 46
Indian economy, liberalisation of xiii
Indian freedom movement 39
Indian National Congress 39–40, 77
Industrial capitalism x
Industrialisation 38, 48–49
Inequality in society, violence due to 34
Innocence, end of 34–39
Institutions of knowledge 46, 53
Insurgencies 32, 42
Intellectual murders 91
Intimidation, power of x, xvi, 62, 73, 115, 125, 128, 132, 135, 141

Jews in Europe 5–6
Jha, Bhagyesh 66, 87
Jnanamarga, concept of 52–53
Joshi, Anil 95, 101–2, 104

Kabir, Saint-poet 48–49
Kalburgi, M. M. 101, 103–04, 122–23, 125
development of modern research 91
investigation of case of assassination of 125
murder of 90–95, 104, 116
atmosphere of fear caused by 126
Prof. Kalburgi Hatya Virodhi Samithi of Karnataka 104
writings of 92
Karmamarga, concept of 51–53
Khatri, Yakub 70–72
Kikiyari 56, 66
Killer, dehumanisation of 32

Knowledge *(jnana)* x, xiii, xv, 3–4, 16, 18, 19–21, 34, 36–38, 46, 49, 51–53, 92, 121
Koraj Hill 57–58, 60
Krishna, Lord 17–19, 21, 50, 52–53
Krishnamurti, J. 34, 38
Kumar, Keshav 61, 65–66, 87

Land transfer, deed for 79
Language diversity procession 109
Language, power of 31
Lankesh, Gauri 91, 122, 126–27, 129, 131
Legal systems 46–47
Lending of money, regulations for 79
Literary assassinations 91
Local self-government, principle of 42
Lok Sabha 96, 111

Mahabharata
  Arjuna–Krishna dialogue 17–19, 21
  philosophical thought relating to death 17
Making easy money, idea of 87
Malnutrition, of the Korku tribals 84–86
Mann, J. John 23–24
Marketing of violence 28
Marx, Karl x, 133, 138
Masculine state, notion of 39–43
Mauzo, Damodar 117, 120
Media deterioration 141
Media, entertainment, and advertisement 45
Medical science 4, 16, 23
Medieval literary movement 100
Mein Kampf 13
Merton, Robert 6–7
Micro-credit scheme, for tribals 77, 81
  and money lending system 78
  Self Help Groups under 78, 81–82
Militant tribal movements 88
Ministry of Information and Broadcasting 132
Mob-militancy, of Rathwa tribals 80
Modernity x, 48, 80
Moneylenders 72, 75–76
  books of accounts 79
  dependency of politicians on 76
  Hindu moneylenders 88
  militant tribal movements against 88
  moneylending business 72, 76
  money lending system 78
  Muslim moneylenders 73, 77, 88
  power of 76
  rate of interest charged by 78
  small-time 81
Morality 20, 34
Moral philosophy and ethics 4
Munghate, Pramod 102, 121
Mutual collaboration, principle of 133

Nandy, Ashis 32
  Intimate Enemy 47
Narrative of violence 3
Nation xi, 2, 29, 33, 38–40, 42, 85, 94, 112, 139–40
National Bank for Agriculture and Rural Development (NABARD) 75
Nationalism 40, 99, 111
Nationalism, philosophy of 40, 99, 111
National Socialist (Nazi) party 12
Natural instinct for violence 26
Naxalism, spread of xii
Nivrutti, concept of 50
Nomads, atrocities on 43
Non-cooperation 47
Non-State party terrorism x
Non-violence x, xv, 18–19, 22, 47, 49, 52, 53, 119, 134–40
Nuclear conflict ix–x

Okkund, M. D. 115, 126
Oppressed castes, violence against 45
Orsang river 57–58, 81

Padmashree, civilian honour of 95
Panchmahals 60, 62, 69, 74, 82–83
Pansare, Govind 91, 101–04, 114, 117, 122, 124–25, 127
Panvad village
  communal riots in 63–64
  congregation of tribals at 64
  deforestation of the low hills 80
  location of 64
  Muslim businessmen in 64
  persecution of Muslims in 68
  sociology of 80
Parliamentary system of government 40–41
  and governance by people 42
Parmeshwara, G. 116
Partition of India xi
PEN Congress xvii, 135
PEN International xvii, 134, 140
Philosophy of violence 17
  Arjuna–Krishna dialogue on 17–19
  in Indian culture 17–19
  in Western culture 20
Police 'encounters' 32–33
Political assassinations 3
Political network 39
Political power
  decline of 58
  of Hitler 6
  of Jews in Europe 6
  masculine 41
  supported by an army and a police force 41
Political violence
  architects of 33
  assassinations of political rival 3
Politics of crime 36
Positive aggression, idea of 5
Positron Emission Tomography (PET) 24
Poverty 6–7, 24, 33, 38, 86
Pravrutti, concept of 50

Progressive Writers 133
Progress–violence relationship 34
Psychological disorders 4, 37
Purushatva, notion of 47

Quality of violence 32
Quit India movement 140

Racial inequalities 141
Radical ideologies, of tribals 88
Rathwa, Arjun 68, 73–74
Rathwa tribals, mob-militancy of 80
Religious fundamentalism 141
Religious institutions 26

Sadhana 102, 118
Sahitya Akademi 92–97, 99, 103–04, 107, 125
Sahitya Parishad 104, 110
*Sahukar*s 74, 76
  and institution of *sahukari* 88
Saint-poets 48, 100
Sampurna Kranti Vidyalaya 106, 110
Sangh Parivar 68
Sankhya school of philosophy 51
Sarva-Bhasha-Samvad 113
Sattva 51
Satyagraha 47, 105–06, 135
Scheduled Caste 132
School
  school children, in India
    destruction of childhood in name of education 38
    document certifying learning 35
    education loads in minds of 37
    ethos of violence in 36
    ideal way of educating 35
    knowledge transfer 34
    period of childhood 37
    pressure to succeed 35
    profession of teaching and 35
    psychological burden of violence 34
    school dropouts 39
    sense of confidence 36
    social space and privacy of homes 37
    tuition classes 35
    violent school system and 39
    school dropouts 39
Sedition case 132
  on folk singer in Tamil Nadu 100–01
  Indian law related to 95
Self-absorbed violence 23
Self-glorification, obsession with 141
Self-Help Groups (SHGs) 78, 81–82
Selfhood, notion of 41
Self-immolation 23
Sense gratification, philosophy of 19–20, 22, 45
Serotonin 5, 30
  brain's capacity to produce 24
  as cause of suicide 24
  flow inside the brain 23
Sevagram Ashram 129
Sexual violence 10–11

Sickle cell anaemia 67, 83–84, 86
Sin, concept of 16
Social
  aggression 6
  behaviour 24
  conflicts in Indian culture 46
  inequality 46
  morality 34
  norms 9, 47
  relations 31
  structure 9, 19, 43–46
Socialising, violence due to 34
Socially transformative literature 120
Social structure, effect on violence 43–46
Sociology xiv, 4, 6, 16, 25, 80
Socrates 9–10, 90
Sovereign rights of tribals, over the forests 74
Speech, freedom of 101, 134
Spiritual
  evolution 21
  formations 25
State surveillance, of their own citizens x
Sthitapragnya, concept of 50
Stritva, notion of 47
Sudharela 59
Suicides
  due to
    depression 24
    lack of serotonin 24
  in India 22–23
  method of treatment 24
  suicidal thoughts 24
Supreme Court of India 32–33

Tagore, Rabindranath 38, 90, 114, 134
Tamasa 51
Teaching in India, profession of 35
Technological civilisation 49, 53
Tejgadh village 56–57
  architecture of 57
  communal riots 61–63, 72
  Hindu merchant class at 59
  historical fortification 58
  Koraj Hill 57–58, 60
  layers of habitation 57–58
  lifestyle of 57
  Limdi Bazaar 59, 62, 68
  location of 57
  micro-credit scheme for tribals in 77
  Muslim population in 61–62
  persecution of Muslims in 68–73
  political power, decline of 58
  population of 57
  practice of worship 57
  public places of worship in 59–60
  sarpanch of 70
  Taluka Development Office 59
  Tribal Academy at 65
  village panchayat 59–60
  village ponds 58
  water supply for domestic use 59
  Yakub Khatri episode 70–72
Tendencies towards violence 25–26
Tendulkar, Vijay xii

Thakur, Upendra 22
  History of Suicide in India, The 22
Theological orthodoxies, rise of 116
Tilak, Balgangadhara 21, 51–53
  Gita Rahasya 20, 50
  understanding of the Gita 51
Tribal habitat, devastation of 81
Tribal militancy, reasons for 83
Tribals
  attack on policemen 87
  attitude towards State formation 82
  economic development of 78
  economic empowerment of 76
  elected representatives of people 76
  foodgrains bank scheme for 85
  genetic cell disorder among 83–84
  guerrilla warfare 88
  indebtedness, problem of 78–80
  labourers, migration of 60–61
  languages and culture of 76
  malnutrition, cases of 84
  micro-credit scheme for 77
  mob-militancy 80
  peasants 76
  poison-tipped bows 87
  radical ideologies of 88
  resistance movement 74
  Self-Help Groups (SHGs) 78, 81–82
  social code in matrimonial alliances 82
  socio-economic situation of 67
  underdevelopment and chronic indebtedness 76
  use of bows, arrows, and guns by 80, 87
  in western India 65
  women's status, social transition of 82
Tribal women, violation of 64, 83, 86
Trump, Donald 115, 139
Tukaram, Saint 9, 10, 90
Types of violence 25, 28

United States of America 40
Untouchable caste 6

Vachanas of Lingayat saints 104
Vajpayee, Atal Behari 85
Vemula, Rohith 132
Vidya Vardhak Sangh 103, 115, 123
Village panchayats 59–60
Violence
  factor behind violence 1–2
  in animal world 27
  arises out of desire 47
  classification of 25, 28
  commodification of 28
  countering xi, 46–53
  in mainstream cinema 36
  marketing of 28
  production and management of 28
    symbolic transaction of 28
  against women and children 45
Violence on the self, psychological tendency to inflict 23

Violent emotions, aggression of 5, 27
Violent persons 5, 31
Violent scenes, in films; *see* Indian cinema, violence in
Violent tendencies in nature, evolution of 27
Virtual reality 31
Vivekananda, Swami 54n14
Vora Committee Report 39
Vote banks 76

Western
- culture 17, 20, 22
- knowledge system 19
- medical science 16
- science and technology 19
- society and technology 15

Wife-killing, practice of 45
Wild animals, violence of 26, 33
Women, exploitation of 10, 83
World Bank 49
World Health Organization (WHO) 49
World Trade Organization (WTO) 49
World War I 12
World War II 5, 140
Writers' discontent, towards the State 95–96
- award returning phenomenon 95–96
- decision to return their awards 95
- Government's request to take back the awards 96
- list of the writers who had returned their awards 97–98
- meaning of 99–100
- Parliament response toward 96–99

Zola, Emile 6